C000054379

Commercial Due Diligence

Commercial Due Diligence

A guide to reducing risk in acquisitions

DENZIL RANKINE

FINANCIAL TIMES
PRENTICE HALL

PEARSON EDUCATION LIMITED
128 Long Acre, London WC2E 9AN
Tel: +44 (0)171 447 2000
Fax: +44 (0)171 240 5771
Website: www.pearsoned-ema.com

First published in Great Britain 1999

© Denzil Rankine 1999

The right of Denzil Rankine to be identified as author
of this work has been asserted by him in accordance
with the Copyright, Designs, and Patents Act 1988.

ISBN 0 273 63971 4

British Library Cataloguing in Publication Data
A CIP catalogue record for this book can be obtained from the British Library.

All rights reserved; no part of this publication may be reproduced, stored
in a retrieval system, or transmitted in any form or by any means, electronic,
mechanical, photocopying, recording, or otherwise without either the prior
written permission of the Publishers or a licence permitting restricted copying
in the United Kingdom issued by the Copyright Licensing Agency Ltd,
90 Tottenham Court Road, London W1P 0LP. This book may not be lent,
resold, hired out or otherwise disposed of by way of trade in any form
of binding or cover other than that in which it is published, without the
prior consent of the Publishers.

10 9 8 7 6 5 4 3 2 1

Typeset by Boyd Elliott Typesetting
Printed and bound in Great Britain

The Publishers' policy is to use paper manufactured from sustainable forests.

About the author

Denzil Rankine is chief executive of AMR, Europe's leading specialist in commercial due diligence.

Denzil studied law at the University of Kent and then, after two years with R. K. Carvill in reinsurance broking, moved into consultancy. In 1983 he joined PBD, a small business development research consultancy specialising in helping British companies enter the US market. Over the following four years he played a leading role in growing the business and at the same time visited 49 states in the USA.

In 1987 Denzil was invited to join the Seer Group, a management consultancy which had broken away from Deloitte & Coopers. Denzil founded the strategic research consultancy division of Seer, which worked alongside the corporate finance group. A number of Denzil's clients were in the defence electronics industry; as the disastrous nature of Ferranti's acquisition of ISC unfolded, Seer responded, becoming one of the first consultancies to offer a specialised commercial due diligence service. Denzil founded AMR in 1991.

AMR

AMR is a strategic research consultancy based in London. It was founded in 1991 and is Europe's leading specialist in commercial due diligence. AMR has investigated over 400 transactions on behalf of British, American and continental European acquirers in 26 countries. The value of these transactions ranges from £1 million to £800 million. AMR has also investigated a number of multi-billion dollar cross-border mergers.

AMR's consultants have on average eight years' strategic research experience, gained after earlier careers in operational roles. All are fluent in at least one language other than English.

AMR's clients include one of the world's top five media groups, France's largest electronics group and one of Britain's largest distribution companies. AMR's corporate clients are mostly capitalised at over £1 billion, but AMR also works with a wide range of other smaller public and private companies. In the private equity field, AMR works for many of the top private equity firms.

The author may be contacted at the following address:

Denzil Rankine
Chief Executive
AMR International Limited
Mutual House
70 Conduit Street
LONDON
W1R 9FD

Tel: 020-7534 3600
Fax: 202-7534 3636
E mail: denzil@amr.co.uk

Contents

Executive summary

Commercial due diligence (CDD) helps acquirers and investors to decide whether or not to commit their resources to a transaction.

Essentially, CDD is a mini-strategy review of an acquisition target. It is not a replacement for financial due diligence (FDD); it complements traditional financial investigations, particularly as it can highlight the key issues impacting future profitability.

CDD comprises the analysis of three key areas:

1 Market

2 Competitive position

3 Management.

CDD can be conducted with or without the knowledge of the business under review. Hostile acquisitions and early-stage acquisition proposals apart, it is best conducted 'vendor aware'. The CDD team must retain an impartial relationship with the seller and ensure that the news of a potential change in shareholding structure is not spread around the market.

Although published information can be useful, the main focus of information-gathering should be among contacts close to the target company; these will include customers and suppliers. It is sometimes possible to interview former employees and competitors. To obtain useful results from these contacts, detailed planning is required in the areas of:

- Defining what is critical to the business.
- Working out how best to approach knowledgeable contacts.
- Asking them the right questions.

As most of the CDD process is conducted externally to the target business, the management element of CDD is not achieved through structured internal interviews and tests, but is based on the analysis of discussions with customers and other key market participants.

The quality of the result will depend largely on the quality of information gathered. The subsequent analysis, although strategic, need not be over-complicated. A well worked through SWOT is an excellent starting point.

The output of CDD is a decision on whether or not to make the acquisition or investment. The results of CDD should be practical; the team should be able to answer the chairman's question – 'Would you put your own money into this?'

Beyond the simple yes/no decision, CDD helps acquirers and investors in three key areas:

1 Valuation

2 Negotiation

3 Integration planning.

CDD should provide a clear knowledge of market conditions and the business's competitive position. This information can be fed into a valuation model and should make an accurate assessment of future profitability possible. After all, historical data is no guarantee of future performance.

Negative issues which arise from CDD can be used in negotiation, either to change the terms or to re-structure the deal.

In areas where CDD identifies weaknesses in product, organisation or management, the information gathered from the market should be input to the integration plan. These integration issues impact on profitability and consequently the value of the business.

CDD can be conducted by the acquirer or investor or by consultants. Outsiders are often used for their impartiality, ability to cover a lot of ground quickly and their understanding of how to get the most out of the process. As with using any consultants, much depends on choosing the right organisation.

CDD is used to reduce risk. CDD helps investors and acquirers to put the right price tag on a business and it helps plan how it can be managed.

Introduction

DEFINITION

Commercial due diligence is the investigation and analysis of a company's market, its competitive position in that market and its management ability.

DEVELOPMENT OF CDD

Until the 1990s acquirers devoted disproportionately limited resources to understanding the markets into which they were buying and to analysing an acquisition candidate's competitive position within them. They looked at the numbers and trusted the views of management. Then in 1989 Ferranti bankrupted itself when it acquired ISC without having investigated the company's customer base – this case study at the close of the 1980s acquisition boom marked a turning point in acquisition thinking.

As markets become ever more competitive and acquisition premiums rise in the business cycle, acquirers have to depend more on making their acquisitions grow than on Hanson-style cost-cutting. This has made market understanding and strategic analysis all the more important. At the same time, the major audit-based firms have become increasingly reluctant to provide forthright conclusions to their financial due diligence in the interest of avoiding litigation. Consequently, many investors and acquirers now agree that it is commercial due diligence which tells them if the company will fit the bill. As well as being the analysis on which they base their final decision, CDD also provides major inputs to valuation, the negotiations and to integration planning.

This management briefing offers a detailed and practical exposé of how a rigorous approach to CDD helps acquirers to negotiate better, reduce risk and avoid disasters.

RELATIONSHIP WITH OTHER FORMS OF DUE DILIGENCE

Commercial due diligence forms part of the overall due diligence process. The main three elements of due diligence are commercial, financial and legal. Each of these three requires a separate set of skills and focuses on different aspects of the business. Financial and legal due diligence focus largely on verifying the quality of the business as presented. Commercial due diligence also analyses the current business, but its main purpose is to go further and to assess future performance.

Figure 0.1 sets out the three main types of due diligence and their relationships with the various secondary areas of due diligence.

Fig. 0.1   Relationship between types of due diligence

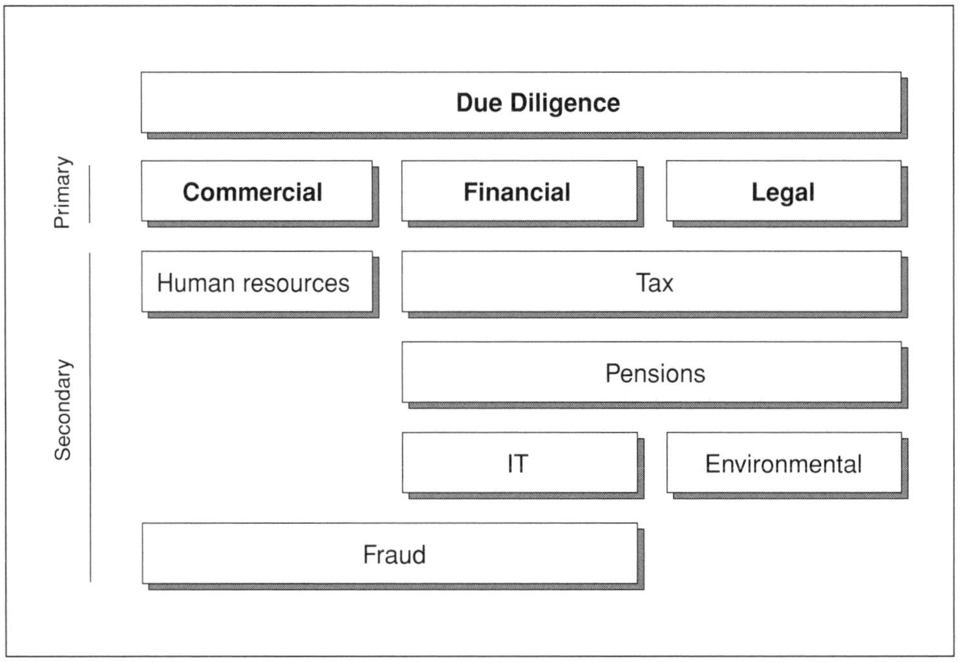

The three main due diligence streams are normally run in parallel, although they do not all have to start and finish at the same time. In the case of a major acquisition, the director responsible for the deal should appoint a team leader for each of the three main areas. They can then conduct whatever investigations are required in the secondary areas of due diligence.

The importance of the secondary areas of due diligence varies by market. In the engineering sector environmental due diligence may be of primary importance; in retail IT is inevitably critical.

THREE BUILDING BLOCKS OF COMMERCIAL DUE DILIGENCE

A company is acquired not for its historical performance but for its ability to generate profits in the future. Commercial due diligence, more than any other pre-acquisition work, allows the acquirer to understand how an acquired company will perform.

Figure 0.2 demonstrates the individual impact on future profitability of the three key elements of commercial due diligence:

- market

- competitive position

- management.

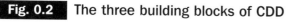

Fig. 0.2 The three building blocks of CDD

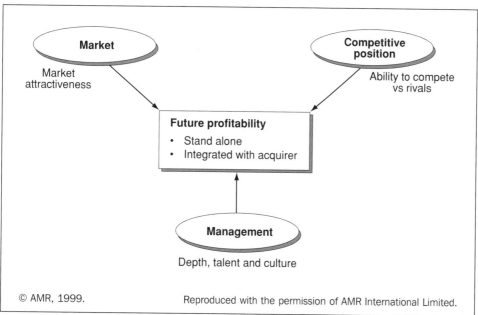

© AMR, 1999.   Reproduced with the permission of AMR International Limited.

Market

Companies which are already active in a market and which are acquiring to build share should know their market well and can use their existing knowledge and analysis – that is assuming it is not out of date, biased or just plain wrong. Private equity investors and companies acquiring into unfamiliar markets need to understand market prospects in detail.

Competitive position

The competitive position of the target is fundamental to its future performance. A target market may well be attractive, but there is no guarantee that an acquisition candidate will perform in line with the market.

> For example, AT&T may have been right to consider entering IT due to its obvious high growth and the convergence of telephony and computing. But NCR, billed as the entry card to IT, was a fundamentally uncompetitive business in IT. AT&T entered a growth market by acquiring NCR, but it paid dearly for NCR's lack of competitiveness.

Management

Management can be just as important in delivering profits as the products or services sold. Unless a business is being acquired purely for its assets, any acquirer must assess management ability in its own right, compared to competitors and compared to the acquirer. It is difficult to believe that the strait-laced Japanese companies Sony and Matsushita considered the management challenge in sufficient detail before acquiring the free-wheeling Californian studios, Paramount and Universal.

CDD should provide excellent insights to management, but it is not a substitute for formal management appraisal methods. Given the structure of the process, possibly only 5–10 per cent of a CDD team's time can be practicably spent assessing management, but the value of the output can far outweigh that of the market and competitive position elements.

For example, a niche British medical equipment company had identified the German market leader in the same niche as an attractive and inexpensive acquisition. CDD revealed that the company dominated its market niche but customers and suppliers were aware that the company was over-reliant on its egotistical owner. The owner later admitted to the external CDD team that his intention was not just to be acquired, but to show the acquirer how he could run the UK operations better. The deal was abandoned.

The focus of this briefing will be to set out step by step how these three building blocks are combined to provide acquirers with a clear understanding of how an acquisition candidate will perform.

When is CDD needed?

AT WHICH STAGE OF THE ACQUISITION PROCESS?

Commercial due diligence refers to the pre-acquisition investigation of a company. This means that there is at least an outline acquisition agreement, a letter of intent or heads of agreement.

Alternatively, some acquirers use a commercial due diligence investigation at an earlier stage in their acquisition process.

For buyers the commercial investigation of companies and markets is an ongoing process; acquirers should constantly monitor markets and target companies which are of interest to them as this prepares the way for the detailed investigation required during CDD.

Figure 1.1 shows four stages of the acquisition process and the level of detail required on acquisition candidates.

Fig. 1.1 When to do CDD?

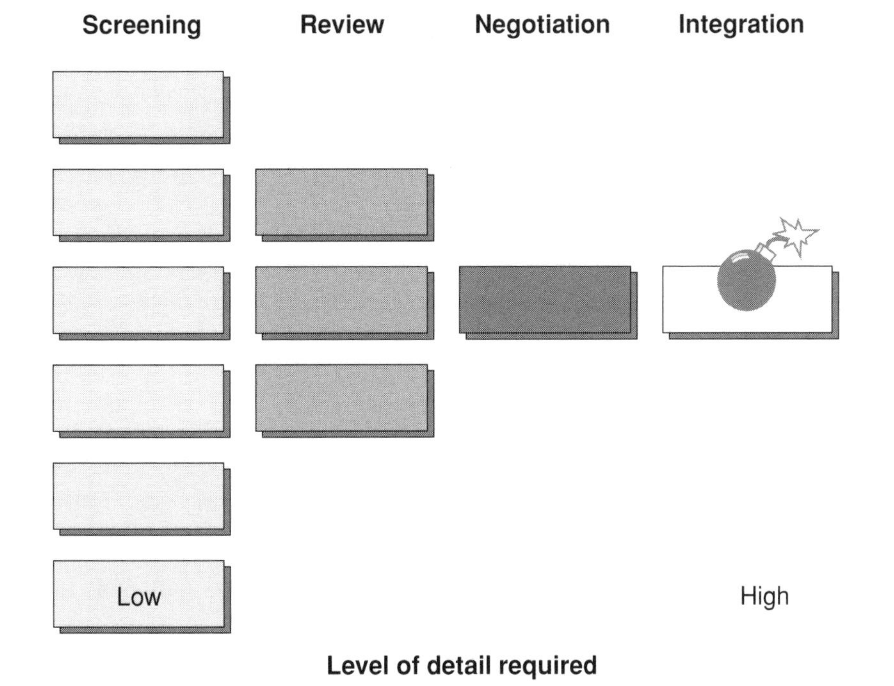

Screening   Review   Negotiation   Integration

Low   High

Level of detail required

© AMR, 1999.   Reproduced with the permission of AMR International Limited.

Table 1.1 Level of investigation by stage of deal

Stage	Level of investigation
Screening	A small amount of information is required on a large number of targets which are identified as possible acquisition candidates; this is not due diligence.
Review/target evaluation	More detailed information is required on a small number of businesses, which may not be declared sellers at this stage; pre-deal due diligence can be very useful.
Negotiation/heads of agreement	The formal due diligence phase.
Integration	Too late to conduct due diligence! This was the approach which bankrupted Ferranti.

There are merits to conducting a detailed target evaluation, or pre-deal CDD, of targets during the review phase. These are:

- CDD is the least expensive type of investigation to commission from specialist consultants. It can also provide a clear pre-acquisition stop–go decision.

- CDD can be conducted without the knowledge of the target. This provides an independent review of the business and does not raise the seller's expectations. It avoids embarrassment if the proposed acquisition opportunity is not progressed.

- If the acquisition is considered attractive, the potential acquirer is well armed with information on the business. This can be invaluable in building a strong relationship with the seller and in leading the negotiations.

For example, a UK listed heavy engineering group owned a hospital monitors subsidiary. Over dinner the group's chairman indicated to a counterpart from a group better known for its medical division that his subsidiary might be acquirable. Hospital monitors is a highly attractive market. The company's financial performance was no more than average, but it was apparently set to improve.

The potential acquirer commissioned pre-deal CDD. The investigation uncovered a series of management blunders, the worst of which had misdirected new product development. The company could not match any of its competitors' new-generation, multi-channel, user-friendly monitors.

The company was starting to lose market share as its monitors were being replaced by competitors in key accounts. It was on the point of suffering further margin pressure as its products were beginning to appear undifferentiated. The situation would only get worse.

IS CDD NEEDED AT ALL?

Although CDD is an excellent method of reducing risk, it is not essential for every acquisition. If, for example, you have the opportunity to acquire the remaining shares in a joint venture, you should already have an excellent insight into the market, into management and into the business's competitive position, although you may well question why your partner is selling out.

CDD is particularly necessary when the acquirer has little information on the key commercial aspects of the target business. Therefore, the level of information already held on a business will be one of the factors determining the scale and focus of investigations.

After information, the second factor is risk. The need for CDD increases in proportion to the level of commercial and financial risk. The areas of greatest risk vary between acquisitions. In some cases it may be competitors, in others it may be integration difficulties. The acquirer should gauge each of the major risk areas within the three building blocks of CDD – market, competitive position and management – and ensure that each one is sufficiently well understood.

Therefore the decision whether or not to conduct CDD is based on a business judgement of the balance between risk and knowledge. This often manifests itself as the need to convince a sceptical board.

Figure 1.2 provides a simple framework for deciding whether CDD is necessary.

In the 1980s and 1990s, many acquirers made an over-optimistic judgement of this balance between risk and knowledge. In numerous cases the decision not to use CDD had disastrous results.

Fig. 1.2 Assessment of when CDD is necessary

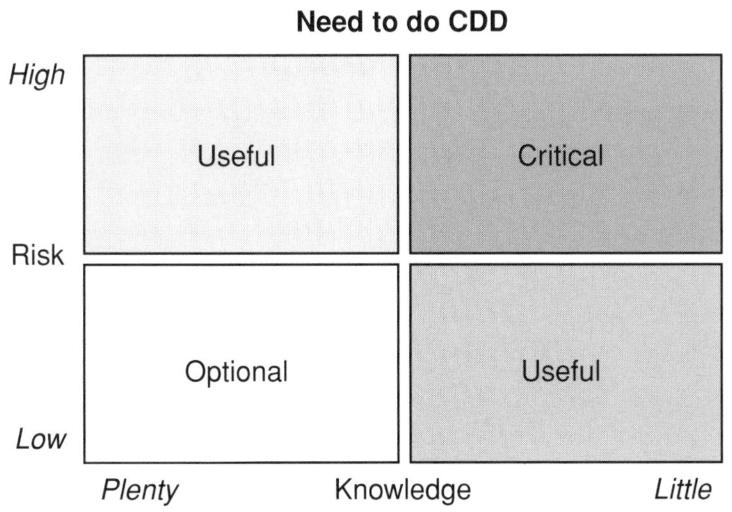

© AMR, 1999.   Reproduced with the permission of AMR International Limited.

For example, Bunzl made 40 acquisitions in 1989, with no more than minimal CDD. Subsequent profit and share price collapses led to the management being ousted. The new team has since focused on understanding markets before investing. BET followed a similar path at the same time and new management was brought in during the early 1990s to sort out the mixed bag of businesses which it had acquired. It never recovered investor confidence and later succumbed to Rentokil's hostile bid.

Once the decision has been made to conduct CDD, the acquirer needs to be clear about its parameters and objectives. The next chapter deals with these topics.

2

Preparation and defining parameters

DEFINING YOUR GOAL

A poorly defined commercial due diligence programme can lead to over-paying, integration difficulties or plain disaster.

The most commonly made mistakes are to focus on the wrong issues or to use erroneous information.

> For example, when Malev, the Hungarian airline, was desperate to start the modernisation of its fleet it made a small acquisition principally for the seller's three Boeing 737s. Carried away by the excitement of the deal, it never occurred to Malev's managers to ask the right questions. Malev subsequently found that each plane had different seating configurations, different maintenance schedules and different cockpit instrumentation. Substantial additional investment was required to sort out the mess.

From the outset of any CDD programme, you should make sure that you can answer the following questions:

- Why are we planning to buy this company?
- Are we looking at the market, the company, management or all three?
- What are our parameters?
- What is our single most important objective?
- How will we handle the seller and its customers?
- How will the results be used?
- How will this commercial work relate to other due diligence investigations?

Why are we planning to buy this company?

Acquisition is an excellent market entry method but a CDD programme differs to a market entry study. The critical success factors for a market entry are very different to those for an acquisition because they focus heavily on barriers to entry. A market entry study analyses the market as a whole and individual segments are evaluated to determine the level of potential opportunity they may hold.

A CDD programme concentrates to a great extent on a specific company. The market is reviewed, but it is defined by the target company's standpoint. A particularly strong emphasis is placed on the company's ability to compete within that market. Equally, the CDD programme should highlight major integration issues.

The key focus of a CDD programme will inevitably be the decision whether or not to acquire. In the event of a negative result other issues should be considered.

These could include finding alternative attractive targets, considering joint ventures or organic growth.

If the acquisition is intended to achieve economies of scale, knock out a troublesome competitor or add management skills then the CDD team must understand this clearly so that it can determine whether the proposed acquisition will deliver the desired result.

Are we looking at the market, the company, management or all three?

Balance the emphasis on these three aspects according to risk. It is a common mistake to confuse market and competitive position and lump them into a single category. Equally, management is sometimes left off the agenda by acquirers who are unfamiliar with how CDD can provide valuable information in this area.

What are our parameters?

Fundamentally, CDD is a mini strategy review of a target company.

The parameters of CDD must be more detailed than just a description of the product or market and the naming of specific countries. It is essential that the CDD programme addresses all areas of risk and areas where there is insufficient information. The parameters must also take integration planning into account.

Sometimes sellers, or their advisors, attempt to restrict the parameters. For example:

'You can't have access to top management – it's too sensitive.'

'You can't talk to our clients.'

'Don't bother looking at that competitor – they are very weak.'

Any of these should sound alarm bells.

For example, the management of a market-leading British engineer which was for sale told the acquirer's CDD team that it had only one real competitor. The CDD team ignored this advice and interviewed other rivals. It found that one supposedly weak German competitor had just received major investment from its parent and was committed to reducing its manufacturing costs and to new product development. It was set to launch a new technology at the next major trade show and it then planned to target the British engineer's customer base.

Equally, it is essential to assess management as the acquirer will depend on them to run the business. An acquirer can rarely afford to have management walk out.

The acquirer should first set its parameters; then it can address sensitivities and the difficulty of obtaining information. CDD experts can nearly always find a way around sensitive issues and problems of access.

What is our single most important objective?

The best results are achieved by sticking to a clearly defined objective such as 'We need to establish what precisely the benefits of buying this company would be'.

The CDD team should focus on this central objective, but as the programme progresses it will most probably be asking a modified set of questions. The two most common mistakes for a CDD team to make are to remain too rigid in its approach or to be distracted by detail. Almost every CDD programme will inevitably cover a wide range of issues, and the focus will change as the reality of the target's position within its market unfolds and as management issues arise. Every time the programme becomes more tightly focused or is redirected due to unforeseen events and opportunities, make sure that the team keeps its eye on the ball.

A useful technique to ensure that the team remains focused on the single most important objective is to challenge the team during the process with the 'chairman's question'. This is the simple question which the hurried chairman asks. It tends to be direct – for example:

'Would you put your own money into this?'

or:

'Can you give me three good reasons why we should do this?'

Remaining focused on the central objective is more difficult when a CDD programme has a number of objectives. For example:

'Should we enter the widget market?'

and:

'Should we buy Acme-Widget?'

These need to be answered in turn. The second question cannot be answered positively unless the first, market-entry question is positive. To use time and resources efficiently, much of the information-gathering, and even the analysis, can be conducted in tandem. Nonetheless, the team must ensure that any primary objective, such as market entry, has been dealt with satisfactorily before investing the effort in finalising the detail on the second objective.

How will we handle the seller and its customers?

It is difficult to satisfy a mixed audience. The team conducting the commercial due diligence project must be clear for whom the project is being conducted and what their objective is. In cases where CDD is conducted with the knowledge and assistance of the vendor, the CDD team must remain clear that the work is being conducted for the buyer and not for the seller.

In the first instance, sellers often react negatively to the prospect of CDD. Selling a company is a stressful time and due diligence generally knocks the price down. It can even stop the deal. The seller is also wary of any damage CDD will do to his business, as he will have to continue to manage the business during and after the sale process.

Sellers are often very anxious about any contact with their customers. The CDD team should emphasise that change of ownership need not be included in any customer survey. Ideally the results of the CDD programme should be fed back to the seller, whatever the outcome. This provides a positive return for the seller. This subject is dealt with in greater detail at the end of this chapter.

How will the results be used?

As set out later in Chapter 11, negative results are used differently to positive results. The CDD team should know how the results are likely to be used so that they can cover all of the necessary angles.

THE RIGHT LEVEL OF DETAIL

Finding the balance

Not every acquisition decision requires an inordinate level of detail. If the level of risk in a decision is low – buying a different sandwich to your usual one for lunch – then little time and effort can be justified to take that decision. When the level of risk is high – as it inevitably is with larger deals and transactions which are distant from your home market or known product areas – then the level of detail required will increase. Equally, deals which are controversial and split the board will require a lot of justification. The trick is to find the right balance.

In many cases the practical issue of time also comes into consideration.

The danger of too little information

One of the main reasons for misguided decision taking is the lack of high quality information and analysis. This equates to a lack of strategic thinking. Numerous studies, including AMR's (which is Europe's largest survey on the reasons for success and failure in acquisitions, published in *A Practical Guide to Acquisitions* by D. Rankine, Wiley, 1997), show that over 50 per cent of acquisitions fail. In many cases these failures are due to ill-considered strategies where the buyer falsely believed it had pieced together a satisfactory understanding of the market, but in fact it was reacting to an opportunity.

There are many published examples of companies which proceeded with transactions based on too little information.

For example, Quaker encountered serious difficulties as a result of its acquisition of Snapple, a popular soft drink in the USA. High volumes of the product had been sold to Europe. However, a quick look inside the distributors' warehouses would have shown that the shelves remained packed and that the product had not sold well to consumers.

Equally Rentokil launched a successful hostile bid for BET without even counting the number of floors which the company occupied in its head office building. Cost-saving opportunities were less than expected as there were hundreds fewer staff to make redundant than anticipated.

In a US example, Danka failed to understand Eastman Kodak's business and implemented disastrous new sales policies.

Too much information

Is it really possible to have too much information? In some cases, yes. If the buyer is only allowed access to a data room there may be too much information available, albeit within a short time, and it will be difficult to unearth the key issues. When a CDD team gathers too much information it runs the risk of being ignored. Recipients are unable to digest filing cabinets of data; the result can be as dangerous as when there is too little information.

One of the keys to success is to spot what is important, obtain the information which is relevant to those issues and then summarise it coherently. Instruct your team members and consultants to provide a straightforward conclusion and concise summary pages to each section of their reports. Information overload causes executives' eyes to glaze over and they stop taking anything in.

The right amount

The commercial due diligence team should be able to provide the answer, in a sentence. It should then back up its answer, on a page. Plenty of supporting information will be useful and required. The team must be able to demonstrate that it has sufficient supporting information to justify the key arguments behind its answer. There are rarely more than half a dozen of these supporting arguments.

Figure 2.1 provides an indication of the level of information required depending on the reason for the acquisition. It also highlights the focus of enquiries for various acquisition strategies.

Fig. 2.1 **Information and analysis requirements by market and product profile**

	Present	New
Present (MARKET)	**Market penetration** *Information:* Internal sources, little external assistance required beyond customer satisfaction *Analysis:* Use existing models and criteria	**Product acquisition** *Information:* Heavy focus on customer needs, internal sources can often suffice for other data *Analysis:* Extension of internal planning procedures
New (MARKET)	**New market entry** *Information:* Heavy focus on competitive issues as well as customer needs *Analysis:* Tools required to assess critical success factors and barriers to entry	**Diversification** *Information:* Highly detailed review of all market issues required *Analysis:* Detailed analysis of market is required as is an analysis of competitive positioning

PRODUCT

The company's competitive position should be reviewed separately to the market. The investigating team needs to assess where the risks lie and develop a sufficiently solid information base to make an informed decision.

Management

It is rarely possible to obtain too much detail on management. Astute sellers restrict the level of access to management, arguing that they wish to minimise disruption to the business. A CDD team often has only one or two opportunities to meet management; otherwise it must obtain some useful views from its enquiries in the market. The team then has to piece together the little information it has gleaned to build a view of management depth, style and culture.

STAYING OBJECTIVE

It is not always easy for managers reviewing an acquisition to remain dispassionate. Some of the reasons are:

- a successful acquisition can lead to career progression;
- a failure can result in the opposite;
- managers can become too close to projects, falling in love with them;
- few organisations reward managers for saying 'no'.

In some cases, the project champion may be faced with a transformation of his personal circumstances. This makes it even more difficult to remain dispassionate.

> For example, a British trade show organiser was due to acquire the Austrian market leader. The British managing director designate relearnt German, organised to move house to Vienna and arranged local schooling for his children. After dedicating over one year of his time to the deal, he then faced deal-breaking issues in due diligence. He decided to call the other side's bluff, knowing that it would break the deal – which it did. This correct decision consequently threw his personal life into turmoil.

One advantage of using outsiders is that they are more likely to remain dispassionate about the company or market they are investigating. Outsiders will be judged on the quality of their work, not on whether or not they support a certain manager's pet project.

Nor is fending off external pressures easy. Quoted companies can come under pressure for 'doing nothing'.

> For example, Fairey Group plc turned down numerous acquisitions in the late 1980s when rivals were highly acquisitive, but often overpaying. The financial community started to accuse the group of being 'boring'. Fairey then became a buyer in the early 1990s when it could acquire sound businesses at sensible prices. But it did not buy everything it investigated.

Any good business development director will have turned down a number of partnerships or acquisitions, some at the eleventh hour, due to the results of commercial due diligence investigations.

Well-managed groups do not 'shoot the messenger' but reward managers for resisting the temptation to push ahead with ill-conceived acquisitions or marginal ventures. In the long run, staying objective can save organisations a lot of money.

RELATIONSHIP WITH FINANCIAL DUE DILIGENCE

Why should you go to the trouble and expense of conducting detailed commercial due diligence when the financial due diligence investigation can give you the answer anyway?

The reason is because you are not acquiring historical profits, which have been distributed to the seller's shareholders, but you are buying the potential to make profits in the future. A good financial evaluation can cover a lot of ground. Skilled analysis can spot many business issues and can make sensible forecasts about a company's performance and even market trends. However, financial records are by their very nature historical. Although the numbers must be examined, it is the commercial aspects of the business which create future profits.

So it is best to conduct the commercial and financial evaluation of acquisition opportunities in parallel. The danger of ignoring the commercial issues – or at least doing no more than guessing at them from internal information – is that forecasts will hardly be robust. And as your valuation is based on future performance it too will be wrong. This is due to the increasing levels of competition in all areas of business and due to the accelerating speed of change which makes yesterday's news today's ancient history. A cynic could liken relying solely on financial information to using only the rear view mirror when driving along a motorway. As the acquisition decision and the valuation will be based on forecast profits, it is essential to look ahead with as much clarity as possible. That means you should use CDD to inform and improve your financial analysis.

The commercial evaluation team must be tasked with providing as robust a market and product forecast as possible. It is best to start with existing sales data but even when this is not available some useful work can be done on growth drivers. The market and product forecasts must be based on sound market information and analysis, not just an extrapolation of historical performance. Well structured commercial forecasts can then be integrated into the financial model, particularly if a discounted cash flow (DCF) technique is being used. This approach will increase the accuracy and credibility of the financial models.

The commercial investigation of the acquisition target can even provide some information on the cost side. Some basic benchmarks on structure, organisation and perhaps even the cost base is possible during the CDD investigation, particularly if competitors are interviewed. This information can be used to help plan restructuring and cost-cutting; it can also be usefully fed into the financial model.

Obviously the CDD team should liaise with the FDD team. The major accountancy firms recognise this; now ever-fearful of litigation, they welcome independent input. But it does not make sense to use an accountancy firm to conduct CDD; their culture restricts the scope and depth of their investigations as much as does their fear of litigation.

MANAGING YOUR RELATIONSHIP WITH THE SELLER

Emotions can run high

If mishandled, the seller can find due diligence an intrusive and unpleasant experience. Therefore close management of your relationship with the seller is important and requires sensitivity.

The relationship will have two elements:

- conflictual – both sides negotiating hard for the best deal;

- co-operative – planning integration, working out how to run the businesses together.

You need to be aware of these two elements and structure your team and your approach accordingly. The 'good cop' may be responsible for planning integration, while the 'bad cop' negotiates hard on price.

The seller is at least as anxious as the buyer to obtain a positive result from the transaction. If the seller is an entrepreneur as opposed to a corporation, he will be very sensitive as his future personal fortune is at stake. Maintaining close contact with the seller has two advantages. It helps to:

- smooth the relationship so that misunderstandings are avoided and any difficulties which arise can be addressed in a level-headed way;

- assess the calibre of management by monitoring the way in which they manage the process and react to events.

If the seller is a corporation these points remain important but the atmosphere may be less emotional. If corporate sellers attempt to restrict access to the company during the sale process the buyer can use CDD as a useful method of gaining access. The buyer can require a meeting between operational management and the CDD team to set up some customer research.

Many sellers now accept that customer research is a necessary part of the sale process. If they are surprised by this requirement or uncertain about its consequences they can be persuaded of its value on the following basis:

- it is a normal part of the acquisition procedure;
- the survey can be dressed up as a customer care programme;
- change of ownership will not be implied or discussed in the interviews;
- the results will be provided to the seller even if the deal does not go ahead.

An experienced CDD project leader can always persuade the seller that a customer survey will not damage his business. But the CDD team will inevitably look at a wider set of issues – CDD should be used to gain an insight into much more than just customers. For example, management style and ability can be judged by its 'actions and reactions' to the CDD process and to the information it generates.

3

Published information sources

USING PUBLISHED INFORMATION EFFECTIVELY

Any commercial due diligence programme will call on published information to some extent. If you can find pertinent information, or even better information and analysis, which has already been compiled and published in one form or another then the investigation should be plain sailing. Unfortunately this is rarely the case. Even when there is plenty of published information it will never be sufficiently detailed. Competitors do not publish their operational procedures or tactics. Nor do they detail how they add value in each market niche. Equally, customers do not publish their detailed requirements and views of their suppliers.

A major acquisition will require a level of detail and insight far greater than any published source can provide. Often there is plenty of top-level information on overall markets which can be used for background information or for supporting evidence. Inevitably very little of this published information is pertinent to the detail required for the evaluation of an acquisition target's competitive position.

Business development departments and operational managers must establish at least basic systems which collect information on companies in the business arena; these are typically competitors, customers, distributors and suppliers. They should also gather information on the markets served both by their own company and by their customers. In some cases you can be confronted by too much information. Some business development departments become information hoarders in the hope that it could become relevant at some point in the future. If so much information is poorly organised it becomes an incoherent jumble in which the limited quantity of relevant and useful detail is often overlooked.

Published information is most useful for the market evaluation aspect of a CDD programme. Table 3.1 shows where published information is useful.

Table 3.1 Relative usefulness of published information

Aspect of CDD	Usefulness of published information
Market	Useful
Competitive position	Some use
Management	Little use

FINDING THE RIGHT INFORMATION SOURCES

There is a surprising variety of information sources. Some are obvious, others are much more obscure. Experienced business development executives and consultants learn how to find the less obvious information sources which are relevant to an acquisition target and its market and how to get the most out of them. A good approach to finding the best sources is to ask people connected to the industry. Always try the editorial team of the trade magazines. Often they will be able to refer your enquiry to some of the better sources.

If you are particularly lucky some industry contacts may fax you through a few useful pages from a directory, trade publication or industry report which is sitting on their desk.

It is best to keep an open mind as to which sources will be useful. Obviously brokers' reports are relevant when reviewing major markets served by public companies; at the opposite end of the spectrum are the *Yellow Pages* and trade association newsletters.

Sources checklist

Checklist 3.1 sets out some of the best information sources to use.

Checklist 3.1 Published information sources

- Newspapers
- Commercial databases (profound, etc.)
- News clippings services (McCarthy's, etc.)
- News services (Reuters, Bloomberg, etc.)
- General trade directories (*Kompass*, *Kelly's*, *Key British Enterprises*, etc.)
- Specialised trade directories
- *Yellow Pages*
- Buyers' guides
- Published market reports (Mintel, Keynote, Frost & Sullivan, Euromonitor, etc.)
- Brokers' reports
- Trade association handbooks/membership listings
- Trade show catalogues
- Trade magazines
- Government reports and statistics
- Companies House
- Industry regulators
- In-house journals and magazines
- Company brochures and promotional material
- The Internet

There are even directories which can be used to direct you to the best information sources. Two of these are *Benn's Media* and *Willings Press Guide* which list all trade publications. These are worth consulting, but there is no substitute for asking around to assess what is available and what is good.

Assistants at business libraries such as London's Science Reference Library and the City Business Library can also be very helpful.

Is electronic better than paper?

A wealth of information is now available electronically through commercial databases such as Profound, One Source, Reuters, FT Profile and Lexis-Nexis, as well as the Internet. Electronic sources have the advantages of convenience and access.

The quality and depth of information available continues to improve; fortunately indexing and data retrieval methods have also improved. But these commercial databases are far from perfect. The main disadvantages of these services are their incomplete coverage of sources, their lack of detail in niche markets and their cost.

An electronic search on a company which serves niche sectors can yield a very disappointing result. Invariably some useful articles will have referred to the company in question, but they are simply not available electronically – you will need to dig out the relevant journals. Speaking to the editorial staff is a good way of tracking things down – you can then ask the editor to forward a copy of his publication in the post.

Despite their downsides, electronic sources are widely used and can yield excellent results, particularly in major markets. The cost of electronic searches can often be justified by their speed and efficiency. Therefore commercial due diligence programmes should at least start with a review of electronic information sources. However, an organisation that relies for information exclusively on electronic sources is mistaken. It is overlooking excellent additional paper-only published information sources.

The Internet

The Internet deserves special mention, although whatever is written about it today will soon be out of date. The greatest single advantage of the Internet is that it has made access to commercial databases and other information much easier. The Internet is famed for its sheer volume of information, ease of access and low cost. However, it also suffers from less-than-perfect indexing, giving users a lot of irrelevant information and leads, and wasting their time. As predicted by technology experts, access to the Internet has become even easier and more reliable. Search mechanisms are following suit. It is therefore a very useful information-gathering tool.

Obtaining company information

Perhaps the greatest benefit of the Internet is an unexpected one. When seeking a rapid overview of a company, its product information can go a long way. It is no longer necessary to call companies, cope with the question of why a brochure is needed, request that information is sent in the post, hope that it arrives and then deal with an overzealous sales rep demanding to visit you with samples.

Many companies publish information on the Internet which is at least equivalent to their brochures. Some of these companies go further. As the design of the website is often handled by technical staff they do not always recognise the commercial sensitivity of information which is freely available internally. For example, they may not realise just how interesting a full customer list may be to someone investigating their company. The 'golden era' of over-provision of information may now be ending, but nonetheless websites often provide excellent sources of information, some of which might otherwise be slow and difficult to obtain.

THE SHORTCOMINGS OF PUBLISHED INFORMATION

Published information can get a commercial due diligence programme off to a rapid and inexpensive start. But only in the simplest of cases can published information suffice.

Frustratingly, published information is rarely available in the right form. If it exists, it often provides only a 'top-level' market overview which does not break down segments into their various components. This is not surprising. Market reports are targeted at a relatively wide audience and cannot justify the level of detail required by a specialist investigating a targeted company who requires detail on each segment of a market to develop a clear picture of the future prospects of that company and its market.

Understanding the shortcomings of published information allows you to draw conclusions in the correct context. The main shortcomings are that such information may be:

- out of date
- wrong
- incomplete.

Out of date

The 'best before' date of all information is the day it is written, not the day it is sold or the day it is read. This statement is true of this as well as all other publications. In some slow-moving markets being out of date is not a particularly great problem.

> For example, the size and structure of the earth-moving equipment market is not changing anything like as fast as IT markets. Information three years out of date on the world excavator market for a company considering whether it should acquire an excavator bucket manufacturer would still be useful. Information three years out of date on the world dot matrix printer market for a company considering acquiring a manufacturer of printer ribbons would be positively dangerous.

Obviously it is best to obtain up-to-date information. When the best available is out of date it needs to be interpreted with a level of care corresponding to its age.

You can make adjustments to out-of-date information to bring it into line with the current market by applying country or industry growth rates. Adjustments must be made for factors impacting on the market. If these adjustments are considered, the result will be perfectly usable. Importantly, assumptions must be noted so they can be reworked if more relevant information comes to light.

Inaccuracy

Once published, information tends to take on a greater legitimacy. However, not all published information is correct, or even nearly correct. Market reports vary enormously in quality. Even those which are branded by large or well known research houses vary according to the quality of their authors.

In some industries the existence of a published report results in a believable but inaccurate market size estimate being passed around by industry participants. Once the same fiction has been heard from more than one source it becomes accepted as truth. Authors tasked with updating market research reports can be faced with a dilemma if they discover a glaring inaccuracy. What are such authors to do? They have the choice of admitting that their predecessors got it all wrong – implying a possible refund to those who purchased the report and a black mark against the company's brand and reputation – or they can massage the data towards a truer market quantification.

Incompleteness

Many published information sources are incomplete. Some examples are as follows:

- Directories (in many cases) 'advertise' only those companies which have paid a fee; *Yellow Pages* is an exception, but its coverage of the business-to-business arena is highly imperfect.

- Trade show catalogues list only those companies which exhibited; the exhibitor set varies from show to show, and few attract all the top industry players.

- Trade association listings include only member organisations.

- Buyers' guides often include only those companies known to the advertising departments of the publisher.

- Trade journal surveys include only those companies which respond.*

- Published reports often depend on the knowledge of the individual author.

- Companies House depends on businesses being 'limited' and filing their returns.

Note: The author's company, AMR International, was rated by *Management Consultancy* as one of the top strategy firms in the UK, but the survey excluded leading firms such as Boston Consultancy Group and McKinsey!

It is rare that a published information source covers its subject perfectly. Exceptions come in regulated industries. For example, a single directory covers the UK nursing homes sector authoritatively as all nursing homes are government-registered. Its information source is the register. Equally every landfill waste site in the UK is registered.

Given that information sources are typically incomplete you should ask the following basic questions every time you use one:

- How up to date is it?
- Just how accurate is it likely to be?
- How can it be cross-referenced to check its validity?
- How can its inaccuracies be compensated for?

It is often possible to telephone the information source to probe these points further. Trade journalists are fairly accessible; as a rule the arrogance and accessibility of journalists are in inverse proportion to their readership. Authors of trade journal articles are often flattered that their piece has been read and are happy to discuss the subject matter with anyone who shows an interest in it. Market research companies which publish reports will often respond favourably to any enquiries, although of course they will be on the look-out for the opportunity to sell a new report or acquire consultancy work.

CONCLUSION

Published information is the necessary and obvious starting point for any commercial due diligence programme. In well documented industries it can form an important part of the investigation. In poorly documented industries it can be of little use, or downright misleading. It is essential that the shortcomings of published information are well recognised by its users; this will enhance the quality of their analysis.

Once you have got your published information together you can get on with the heart of your work – marketplace investigations.

4

Unpublished information sources

ROLE OF UNPUBLISHED INFORMATION

As we have seen, published information cannot provide a sufficiently detailed insight into a company or a market, so it needs to be supplemented with unpublished information.

Unpublished information comes from asking people questions; it should include interviews in the marketplace. These enquiries should give you excellent information – far better than anything which is published.

Where unpublished information is useful

Unpublished information is most useful for the analysis of the target's competitive position and the evaluation of management quality. Table 4.1 shows where unpublished information is useful.

Table 4.1 Relative usefulness of unpublished information

Aspect of CDD	Usefulness of unpublished information
Market	Useful, particularly in niche markets
Competitive position	Very useful
Management	Essential

The three fundamental problems of availability, quality and being up to date which confound the usefulness of published information can also apply to sloppily collected non-published information.

YOUR OWN ORGANISATION AS A SOURCE

A good first place to start looking for unpublished information is within your own organisation. If you are reviewing a bolt-on acquisition in a market you know well, a lot of information should be freely available, turf wars aside. You can also expect to obtain the full co-operation of colleagues in the interpretation of the information. Once confidentiality considerations have been dealt with, it is helpful to reveal to colleagues that the end objective of the evaluation is an acquisition. This will increase the usefulness of their input.

As organisations often recruit from their competitors, you may have former employees of an acquisition target on your payroll. It is worth looking around within your own organisation to find managers who can provide at least some useful insights to the target and its market. This input can help to direct the commercial due diligence programme and provide leads and contacts.

On the other hand, your own organisation can also be the worst place to look for information. The three problems which you are most likely to encounter are:

- getting hold of it;
- how up to date it is and its quality;
- confidentiality breaches.

Getting hold of it

Information can be difficult to gather as the co-operation of busy colleagues can be difficult to obtain. The status of such an internal enquiry is often low, particularly as managers with profit objectives are under pressure to achieve them.

How up to date it is and its quality

The greatest danger of relying on internal sources for information and opinions on acquisition targets and their markets and management is that this knowledge is often based on past experience and is therefore imperfect. As markets and the competitive positions of players change ever faster, even relatively recent information loses its validity and can become dangerous to rely on.

Also, unless the managers providing you with the market insights are currently involved in the market, it is unlikely that their understanding of a targeted company and its management will be accurate.

> For example, the former IT director of a leading tour operator claimed that the company's complex new system, which was critical to the whole business's performance, delivered its full potential. What he did not know was that over the two years since his departure a series of management bungles had restricted the system's performance.

Obviously, internal sources provide information free of charge, relatively easily and quickly. Be careful not to over-rely on them as they can also be misleading. Use some external enquiries to validate what you have learnt internally.

Confidentiality breaches

Confidentiality can be difficult to maintain within organisations. Most large organisations are less well equipped to deal with confidentiality than professional advisors with strict procedures. Most leaks of confidentiality come from companies conducting their own investigations or from the target, not from professional advisors who are experienced in commercial due diligence.

For example, a speciality chemicals company took a rigorous position on confidentiality during its sale process. It insisted on all of the acquirer's advisors signing a detailed confidentiality agreement. Meanwhile the company's managing director discussed the deal with its biggest customer – and the market was quickly filled with rumours.

Companies are always well advised to establish basic confidentiality procedures. Checklist 4.1 sets out some basic procedures.

Checklist 4.1 Confidentiality procedures checklist

- Allocating code names to individual projects
- Using the code name when referring to the company or market
- Ensuring that appropriate confidentiality undertakings are maintained with every individual and organisation (and its employees and agents) involved in the project
- Maintaining a list of those who are included within the circle of confidentiality
- Briefing everyone in the team and those contacted by the team of the importance of confidentiality
- Using confidential as opposed to shared fax lines
- Locking offices or filing cabinets where confidential documents are stored
- Using appropriate computer security and maintaining the passwords
- Shredding as opposed to binning documents

Checklist 4.1 is basic; it should be expanded for projects where confidentiality is particularly important. While none of the procedures is particularly challenging to set up or maintain, many organisations make the mistake of relaxing procedures either through familiarity or the pressure of time.

OTHER ORGANISATIONS AS A SOURCE

Most of the best information lies within organisations which are in regular contact with the company you are investigating and which operate in that company's market.

Figure 4.1 sets out a pictorial checklist of the various organisations which can act as information sources for a CDD programme.

Fig. 4.1 External information sources

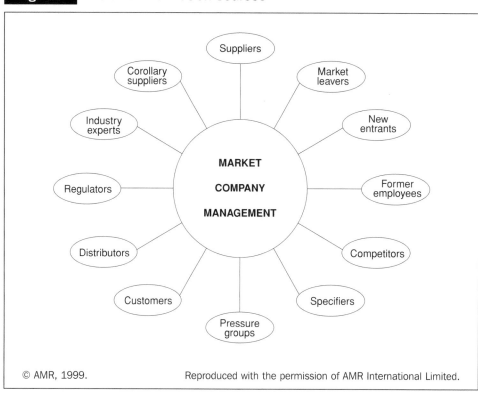

© AMR, 1999.   Reproduced with the permission of AMR International Limited.

Many people are put off by the difficulty of obtaining information from other organisations. In reality more information is readily available to the person who dares to ask, or is able to frame the enquiry astutely, than is commonly thought. Bearing this in mind, the type of information which can be sought from the various market participants is summarised below.

Industry experts

Experts on markets can be found in many different places. These include trade publications, trade show and conference organisers, trade associations, universities, financial organisations (analysts within banks, stockbrokers and insurers) and consultancy organisations.

Usefulness

Industry experts are an obvious first port of call for anyone investigating a company and its market. The ability of experts to provide the level of insight and quality of analysis which you will require of an acquisition target and its industry varies dramatically. For example, experts who are technically minded often focus on their pet topics and the quality of their commercial analysis is questionable. In many cases these experts feel undervalued, so encouragement followed by patience and careful listening are almost always rewarded with some new angles to an investigation and some useful insights into the key issues.

Trade associations are often a frustrating source of information for non-members as the role of associations is to promote the interests of their members. Beyond providing the contact details of their members and mostly useless PR material, they are rarely able to give non-members much useful information.

Access

Many industry experts are happy to share at least some of their knowledge in their chosen field. Particularly in niche markets they may be flattered to be asked and will be prepared to talk at length to strangers. Some experts will try to charge for their advice.

> For example, a British temporary building company was considering an acquisition to enter the German market. A trade journalist had spent five years studying the market and published an annual review of the 200 market participants. Half a day spent with him tapped five years of knowledge and was well worth the modest fee he charged.

Example key questions

- What are the most important changes in this market?
- If you could invest in one company which one would it be?
- How do you rate (target) against competitors?
- Which company is best positioned to add value in the future?
- How would you compare the management styles of the various competitors?

Note: The phrasing of the questions above is direct. Depending on the circumstances of the discussions the interviewer may have to find more subtle ways of phrasing the questions. It is also a good technique to 'bury' the key questions within a wider agenda.

Former employees

Former employees are an often overlooked information source.

Usefulness

Former employees of the company being evaluated can be an excellent source of information. They will have the best insights to the company, its management and the market. There are, however, dangers.

Dangers

The greatest danger of relying on former employees for information is that they can provide you with a biased view. This will depend on the relationship they have with their former employer. One business development director of a major British plc described the former managing director of a company which he was evaluating as a 'very balanced manager with a chip on both shoulders'.

> For example, a small British plc was being reviewed as an acquisition target. It comprised three divisions. Former directors were identified and interviewed from each one. The results were mixed.
>
> *Division one.* The former MD had retired a wealthy man. His greatest interest was to support his son in his new business. He was very happy to provide outsiders with a balanced view of the market.
>
> *Division two.* The managing director had been fired and was very unhappy about the way he had been treated. He was so disgruntled that no real use could be made of the information he provided.
>
> *Division three.* The former sales director was keen to launch a management buy-in (MBI) of his former company. He provided a lot of information, although further verification proved that some of his views were over-optimistic.

Access

Any former employees of the target who have been hired by your own organisation are an obvious starting point. Other such employees may well still be within the industry working for competitors or any of the other organisations set out within this section. You can find them by 'asking around' and by scanning the trade press. The names and addresses of all current and former company directors are available through Companies House. The effort required to seek out one or two former employees of the companies you are looking at is almost always rewarded.

Senior former employees can sometimes be found sitting at home contemplating their next career move or acting as consultants. In these cases they may be very willing participants in any type of enquiry which could lead to a consultancy contract or to a job.

Interviewing former employees has a further advantage when the seller limits access to the business. The seller cannot exclude them from your investigation through a clause in the confidentiality agreement.

For example, Graseby Product Monitoring Division was sold in 1997 soon after a round of cost-cutting and a reorganisation. As one of the prospective buyer's CDD investigations unfolded, more and more former employees emerged. Some were with competitors and most of them knew each other.

Former employees of the target company should be no more or less difficult to persuade to participate in a discussion than any other manager would be in the same role. Their willingness to help will depend on the relevance, and quality, of your approach.

Employees recently hired from the company now targeted for acquisition will provide you with the best information. Their knowledge will be up to date. However, they may also retain some loyalties to their former employers and retain contacts with former colleagues – leading to the danger of a loss of confidentiality.

For example, in 1996 one of the trade bidders for Lloyds List (LLP) had a rude discovery when the senior manager it had hired from LLP turned up leading the successful MBI team against which it was bidding!

Example key questions

- What are the greatest challenges facing companies in this sector?
- How well prepared is (target) to meet these?
- If you were running (target) what changes would you make?
- How would you describe board meetings/management processes?
- Who are the best people in (target)?

Suppliers

Every company has suppliers. But their value to a commercial due diligence programme varies.

Usefulness

The usefulness of suppliers as an information source depends on the importance of the market served to the supplier and the importance of the target company as a customer. For example, a car carpets manufacturer will be intimately aware of the trends in the sales of the vehicle models for which it supplies carpets. It will also be well aware of the trends within its customer base and in the overall car market.

Where the products and services supplied to an industry are little more than commodities, suppliers will be able to provide few insights into the markets they serve, or into the participants in that market. For example, people-based service businesses would be difficult to review through suppliers as the main areas of expenditure are payroll, offices, IT and office supplies. There are no useful suppliers to interview.

An exception to this rule comes in the example of a proposed acquisition of an agency specialising in IT contractors. Customer interviews had cast doubt on the professionalism of the agency's account managers. The CDD programme was extended to include the staff it placed, who were in effect its suppliers. They provided sufficient home truths to stop the deal.

As with all information sources, it is important to recognise any possible bias. Suppliers are often reluctant to denigrate their major customers, or to admit to their own declining sales performance. Suppliers may therefore be inclined to provide a positive view of the performance of customers which can turn out to be misleading. Skilled questioning would be required of a supplier to discover that the management of one of its customers is increasingly disorganised, or that volumes sold into a market segment are waning.

Access

It should be fairly easy to persuade suppliers to discuss the industry which they serve. In the case of an enquiry angled from a new market entry perspective, competitive conflict is unlikely to arise. Indeed suppliers should be keen to secure new or existing customer relationships and can be expected to be co-operative.

Also, suppliers are likely to be interested in discussing the markets they serve as this provides them with an opportunity to improve their customer and market understanding. It is rare that someone offers the opportunity to provide an external perspective on their markets.

For example, when investigating potential acquisition targets in the fire extinguisher market a CDD specialist found it unusually difficult to obtain information from the highly secretive companies. However, a wide range of suppliers were delighted to share their views on the market as they had been the subject of constant supplier reduction and price reduction programmes. They were keen to find better ways of serving their current markets or even find new outlets for their products.

If you are buying a competitor you will probably have an existing relationship with common suppliers. These can obviously be leveraged. When these suppliers are encountered during the course of the current relationship some additional topics can be added to discussions. Obviously, some care is required not to make the line of interest in a company or a market segment so obvious that it leads to rumour or distorted information.

Example key questions

- How do you see the prospects for the market?

- Who do you see as the winners in this market?

- Which companies are most demanding of their suppliers?

- What is the culture of the various companies in this industry?

- What innovations are there, and who is leading them?

Corollary suppliers

Where they exist, major corollary suppliers can be an excellent bet. A corollary supplier supplies a product or service to the same customers as does the target company. For example, a propeller manufacturer is a corollary supplier to a ships' engine manufacturer as both supply shipbuilders. This example holds so long as the engine company does not make propellers itself and so long as it does not source propellers and then offer a package to the shipbuilder.

Usefulness

Corollary suppliers are excellent sources of information as they serve the target market you are investigating. They will possibly have encountered the target company and may even have worked on joint projects. The opinions of corollary suppliers should be valued as they will have insights born out of experience of serving the target market.

Access

Companies between whom there is no conflict which are serving or are interested in the same markets stand to gain from sharing their experiences. Therefore once it has been established that there is no conflict of interest, access to corollary suppliers should be relatively straightforward.

For example, the British temporary buildings company (as mentioned on Page 35) was considering German market entry through acquisition. It interviewed the leading temporary toilet supplier. The toilet company supplied its products and services to exactly the same market. As there was almost no overlap between the product offerings both sides gained from the information-sharing exercise.

Example key questions

- What are the main trends in the market you serve?
- What advice would you give to a company in that market?
- How do you compare (target) to its competitors?

Customers

In any evaluation customers inevitably form a vital part.

Usefulness

Obviously, customers are the source of revenue and consequently profits for the target company. Customer needs and behaviour will determine the relative performance of the target and the size and growth of its markets.

Customers should be categorised into three groups as follows:

- current customers
- former customers
- potential customers.

The top ten or twenty current customers by product or service line should be the primary focus of customer enquiries.

In any acquisition evaluation former customers are an excellent category to pursue. By interviewing customers which have stopped buying or which have reduced volumes you can reveal some of the most negative trends within the target company. Former customers help to highlight a wide range of issues such as poor service or loss of competitiveness.

Dangers

Not every customer account will have seen reduced activity or will have lapsed for negative reasons. For example, all parents become former customers of nappies for a good reason. Care should be taken not to overplay changes in volumes; a reduced volume may simply be temporary correction for earlier over-purchasing.

For example, many buyers declined the opportunity to acquire an old-fashioned snack product manufacturer with a declining brand in the UK. To most potential acquirers the company looked like a cash cow at best. However, the product was fast becoming a fad item outside the UK. This was not apparent as export distribution was poor. Those buyers who considered only the former customers in the UK did not see the potential of the business. The single bidder which saw the potential in new markets bought the business. Profits doubled in a year.

For any acquisition evaluation to be deemed thorough it must cover the major lost customers and those customers whose importance has declined over the previous 12 months.

Access

Sellers and their advisors now accept that many buyers will require some kind of customer satisfaction audit. In such cases the work can be easily agreed. It is often best for the seller to be introduced as the 'sponsor' of the survey. There is no need for the people conducting the survey to declare that there is an intended change of ownership of the target company. It can be framed more as a customer satisfaction survey.

In some cases sellers require that the purchaser does not contact customers and they make this stipulation in the confidentiality agreement. Purchasers should not accept this condition. If sellers remain stubborn it should still be possible to negotiate for an independent survey to be conducted; if necessary the seller can agree the question set. If the seller refuses access to customers you should start to wonder what it has to hide.

If you are conducting CDD before formal access has been granted to the target, it should not be too difficult to find ways of accessing customers. Some companies publish customer lists on brochures or list them on their websites. If customers are not known by name you just have to try contacting the likely buyers of the products or services under review. A series of enquiries should lead to the point(s) of purchase. Although this approach is less focused than working through a customer list, it is effective.

Customers can typically be persuaded to discuss their requirements for products and services as it is in their interest to participate in any initiatives which could lead to an improvement in their suppliers. The major problem encountered by inexperienced interviewers is persuading them to give up some time, particularly if there is no prior relationship with the person making the enquiry. It is best to make the discussion interesting to the customer; consider what is important to the customer and share non-confidential information which the respondent will find useful.

Example key questions

- Why do you buy from (target)?

- How does (target) perform as a supplier, rated against competitors?

- Will you continue to use (target)?

- What could (target) do better?

- How do you rate the people at (target)?

Specifiers

In some industries products or services are specified by people who are not the final user. The most common example is architects, who specify building products. Also retailers such as Marks & Spencer specify the manufacturers from which some of their suppliers should source materials.

Usefulness

Where they exist, specifiers can be critical as they can determine the choice of supplier. They can also be responsible for preparing criteria or an overall project specification which can be more or less favourable to certain companies' skills.

> For example, a British legal publisher considering an Indian acquisition discovered that the lucrative government market was dominated by one firm as senior officials specified its unexceptional publications. The specification was reinforced annually by backhanders.

Access

The issues concerning access to specifiers are very similar to those for customers. Charm and persuasion are required as it can be difficult to persuade architects and specifiers of the burning need to discuss products which they typically find less interesting than the design aspects of projects.

Example key questions

- Which are the most suitable products for this application?

- How do the suppliers compare?

- Will you be specifying more or less of this product and supplier?

- How effective are suppliers at promoting themselves to you?

Distributors

Some manufacturers do not have direct contact with their end users; their primary customers are their distributors. The relationship between a supplier and a distributor, and the various tensions in the relationship, tend to differ from those between a supplier and user in a direct relationship. For example, distributors are more prone to complain of lack of support and will always be concerned by the encroachment of any other organisations which have the right to distribute the same product lines.

Usefulness

Where products are sold via distributors (or wholesalers or retailers) these organisations should have excellent insights into the market and the various companies which serve it.

Like former customers, former distributors can be an excellent source of information. When requesting a discussion with a former distributor you can play on their desire to find new product lines to replace those they have lost.

Access

Distributors are often willing to discuss the market they serve with any organisation which may be able to bring new perspectives or even new products. Conversely, in cases where distributors sense a competitive threat and they value the product line and relationship they will obviously be most reluctant to provide any assistance to people making enquiries. Sometimes you can overcome this problem by focusing on distributors of corollary products.

> For example, a South African computer supplies importer and distributor was being reviewed as an acquisition target. Although large and well known, it was failing to serve its customer base as effectively as some of its competitors. Some of the best information on its failings came from the grey importers which were fulfilling the demand gaps left by the official importer.

Example key questions

- How good is your relationship with your principal?
- How would you describe its management style?
- What problems have you encountered – what could it do better?
- How do these products compare to rivals in the market?
- What are the trends for those products in the future?

Competitors

Inevitably competitors are the most difficult category to access. But they also hold the greatest prize.

Usefulness

The best understanding of markets is held by the competitors which serve it. Competitors have hands-on experience, they should have taken the time to analyse their markets. Therefore they will have the best insights into current and likely trends. You will also want to know why they do not plan to acquire the target company, how they have competed with it in the past and how they plan to compete with it in the future.

Access

The trick is to find a way to access the information and analysis held by competitors. The various methods of systemising information collection from competitors were set out in Chapter 4. This requires that contact, for example at trade shows and during job interviews, is turned to your advantage as opposed to being left as a wasted opportunity.

In acquisition investigations, as in most other business development projects such as the launch of a new product or a new market entry, it is not possible for line managers to obtain the required quality of information directly from current or future competitors. A notable exception can be when a company is considering market entry and it is possible that some form of partnership is a likely outcome. In these circumstances, the investigating company can frame an approach based, quite correctly, on mutual interest. This allows initial access to those companies which are potential partners – and if the partnership approach does not work out with that particular company, then little has been lost. But the company launching the enquiry should have gained some excellent insights from its meetings with competitors.

> For example, during due diligence on a US software company specialising in CAD-CAM, the French acquirer used its consultants to visit all of the target's competitors and discuss partnership opportunities. It transpired that the target company had a weakening position and that a joint venture with one of the other competitors was a more attractive market entry route.

In those cases where it is not possible to make an approach based on mutual interest, it is best to set your sights lower, but nonetheless seek to obtain some basic information from the competitors. This is better than nothing and the enquirer may be lucky and end up obtaining more information than was bargained for. Do not forget that sales people, help desks and publicity departments are used to communicating information about their companies. Sometimes their enthusiasm for their product or service can cause them to over-communicate with outsiders, who may not necessarily be customers.

Consultants can be hired to find a way round the problem of access to competitors. Consultants have the advantage of anonymity and do not always have to declare the identity of their client – they are 'conducting a market survey'. As is always the case in selecting consultants, their skills can vary substantially. Some will be excellent at obtaining access to competitors and can provide the level of insight required for robust analysis; others will have a very low 'hit rate' or they may regurgitate their tired view of the market.

> For example, a newly listed Dutch travel data publishing group was interviewed as a key competitor to an acquisition target. The company was very open about its plans and intended development as it was trying to improve its profile in the market. Equally its senior managers were very clear and forthright in their views on key competitors, including the acquisition target, and were prepared to discuss their perceptions of its strengths and weaknesses.

Example key questions

- What are the market prospects?
- What are the most important things to get right in this market?
- How do you compete with (target)?
- How is (target) managed compared to your company?
- What is the greatest challenge facing businesses in this arena?

New entrants

New entrants are not always easy to identify before they make an official announcement. In some cases intuitive guesswork, backed by sound market analysis, has to go a long way. In any event it is also useful to ask a company which, prima facie, should be interested in an acquisition target or a market segment if it is or why it is not.

Usefulness

New entrants lack hands-on experience, but when companies are considering market entry they will have conducted a market review and they will be hungry for information as they will be assessing entry routes. Although the quality of their understanding of the market will not be as detailed as that of a long-established competitor, all of these characteristics make new entrants an attractive source of information.

Access

New entrants have less to lose from speaking to outsiders than established participants in a market. Their hunger for information is greater, and they may consider entering the market through partnership. Therefore, access is normally easier than to competitors.

Example key questions

- How do you assess the prospects in this business?
- What is the best market entry route?
- Which companies are the best to target?
- What do you see as being the critical success factors in this business?
- What position would you ideally like to achieve in three years?

Market leavers

A group or a company which has left a market should not be overlooked.

Usefulness

The decision to leave a market through the sale of a subsidiary or the closure of a business is not easy. The level of anguish and the strategic review leading to that decision will have given senior management a detailed understanding of the market. The quality of their information and analysis is therefore excellent.

Access

As the group or company is no longer involved in the market there is no conflict of interest. In some blissful cases a courteous telephone call can provide a wealth of excellent information from the director who took the decision to leave the market.

For example, Reed International invested heavily but then exited satellite broadcasting. Managers had a very detailed understanding of the sector as the costly decision had consumed much of their time and effort during the preceding months. A company considering investing in a cable franchise was able to gain excellent insights to the alternative markets to terrestrial television from a 40-minute telephone conversation with a Reed executive.

Example key questions

- Why did you leave the market?
- How do you rate the participants – who will be next to leave?
- What advice would you give to a company seeking to enter the market?
- What is the ideal structure for a business in this market?
- What management approach is the best – which companies have it?

Regulators

Governmental bodies regulate some industries; for example, waste disposal sites are closely regulated and registered. The EU is also a regulator; its inability to harmonise standards for fire extinguishers across the EU has guaranteed the survival of numerous brands and models throughout Europe. Thus when fire extinguisher standards are harmonised across the EU the impact on the industry will be fundamental. Industry bodies can also act as regulators in cases where they set industry standards. For example, certain universally accepted standards in the textile industry were first established by trade bodies.

Usefulness

In those industries which are regulated, the regulators can provide essential insights to likely developments. In some rare cases regulators can be persuaded to comment on the performance and possibly the intentions of companies.

Access

Access to regulators is less of a problem than pinning them down to definitive answers.

Example key questions

- What is the current regulatory position?
- How will this change?
- Which companies are best able to operate within this framework?
- Are any companies particularly active in attempting to pressure regulators?
- What advice would you give to companies in this market?

Pressure groups

On rare occasions pressure groups such as Greenpeace can play a role in shaping markets. The growing list of products which are now considered to be environmentally unacceptable are testament to their importance.

Usefulness

In markets where the environmental issues are critical, pressure groups are an essential source of information. It goes without saying that the information obtained from pressure groups will be among the most biased available. The information becomes more useful if it is possible to obtain separate insights which verify their claims and substantiate that the necessary resources are available to back their proposed initiatives. Greenpeace has many more causes than it has money to back them.

Access

Pressure groups are delighted to discuss their fears and aspirations; access is not a problem.

Example key questions

- What are your objectives in this industry?
- Which companies are you targeting most of all?
- How great a change do you foresee in this industry?

Table 4.2 summarises the comparative usefulness of these various sources.

Table 4.2 Comparative usefulness of information sources

	Management	Competitive position	Market
Industry experts			
Former employees			
Suppliers			
Corollary suppliers			
Customers			
Specifiers			
Distributors			
Competitors			
Market entrants			
Market leavers			
Regulators			
Pressure groups			

Key: High ▬▬▬▬ ▬▬▬ ▭▭▭ ▭▭▭ ▭▭▭ Low

WHO SHOULD GATHER THIS EXTERNAL INFORMATION?

Many of the lines of enquiry set out above can be handled by the company seeking to acquire. However, for most acquisition projects the investigating company will lack the resources or skills to obtain sufficiently detailed information from these 'surrounding' organisations; in this event consultants can be used. The question of selection of consultants is dealt with in Chapter 11. Some consultants specialise in commercial due diligence; others are best known for obtaining information in specific markets or they may be linked to accountancy practices.

In any event, you need to select consultants who are able to use a mixture of investigative skill, charm and commercial nouse to obtain detailed information on the acquisition candidate, its management and its market. Then they need to be able to analyse this information.

Checklist 4.2 provides a useful aide-mémoire for the information-gathering process.

Checklist 4.2 Information-gathering process

Have we:

- defined where the risks lie?

- thought through the key questions to be answered?

- briefed our team thoroughly?

- tapped all in-house knowledge?

- identified all relevant published information services?

- addressed key questions with management?

- identified the best information sources in the market?

- asked management about the best sources?

- found a way to access these sources?

- phrased our questions in the most fruitful way?

- revised our issue set during the process?

- liaised with the other due diligence teams?

- ensured that consultants (if used) have remained focused?

Piecing together the jigsaw

FILLING THE GAPS

Many analyses suffer from lack of information, or the lack of information which is accurate. The main aspects to get right are:

- setting the right information objectives at the outset;
- using the most effective approach to getting the information;
- using the most appropriate people to gather the information;
- verifying information as it is collected;
- recognising the information gaps;
- plugging these gaps where possible;
- admitting to the gaps, if they remain unplugged, in the final analysis.

The right information objectives

Even the most experienced business development directors or strategy consultants often find that the information objectives set at the start of a CDD are very different from those which they would have set with the benefit of hindsight.

Every effort must be made to define the correct information objectives when a CDD programme is launched. As set out in Chapter 1, they will reflect a balance of current knowledge and where the risk lies. It is equally important that the information objectives are reviewed as the work proceeds. As a picture of the company, its management and its market emerges, those issues which were considered important at first often melt away as new issues critical to the success of the business become clear.

Using the most effective information-gathering approach

As set out in Chapter 4, plenty of unpublished information is obtainable; the key is to interview the right individual within the organisations surrounding the target and to frame the enquiries appropriately. If you are faced with an information gap it is always worth rethinking your approach and consider whether a different line of attack would get the desired result.

Using the most appropriate people

Responses to enquiries differ depending on where they have come from and how they have been made. For example, you may have conversations with your competitors, but these are very different to those you would have with your customers. Consultants, if they are good, should be able to gain access to companies which may otherwise be difficult to interview. Also acquirers can surprise themselves by marshalling resources and contacts to get better access to information than they might have otherwise thought possible. This topic is dealt with in greater detail in Chapter 11.

Verifying information as it is collected

Information collection and analysis require different skills. However, the greater the experience and the analytical ability of the person gathering the information, the higher the quality of information they can obtain. For example, in a discussion, where inevitably time and the number of favours which can be asked of the respondent will be limited, the skilled information gatherer will know which issues to challenge, when not to interrupt the flow of the discussion and how to stimulate the interest of the other person.

A quick mental check should be made of every piece of information, or figure, as it is obtained. For example:

- I am told that this company employs 200 and that this is its only site, but there are only 25 cars in the car park. How can this be so?
- This typewriter ribbon company appears to be expanding, yet people are using typewriters less. Is it winning market share or does it have another product line?
- This table says that 500 million bananas are consumed in the UK, but only 250 million are consumed in France. These countries have similar populations so how can this be so?

These questions all have one thing in common – common sense. These 'sanity check' questions are not rocket science, but a CDD team which fails to use them can lead an evaluation into serious trouble.

Recognising the information gaps

Inevitably there will be information gaps. Some information does not exist. Some market sizes are not known as they are too ill-defined, too specialist or too small to have warranted the detailed investigation by a market report publisher, or in some cases by the market participants themselves. For example, no one knows precisely the size of the market for CDD consultancy services as it is so fragmented.

When they are important these gaps should be recognised and then efforts can be made to plug them. Do not forget that in all but the smallest markets size can be less important than profit drivers and market growth. Once you have spotted the information gaps it is then critical to recognise which ones are the most important.

Plugging the information gaps

Once all the practicable information sources have been accessed and the remaining information gaps have been spotted, there are two ways to plug them: guesswork and assumption. These are not the same.

Assumptions have to be based on evidence which can be cross referenced. For example, Table 5.1 sets out an example of how a product sales estimate of four competing companies can be arrived at.

Table 5.1 Market for left-handed widgets

Company	Sales estimates (£m)	Comment
Alphatool	5.2	50% of total sales, balance in right-hand market
Betaway	3.8	Last year's results plus 5% growth
Calypso	3.0	50 employees/£60 000 turnover per head
Dinosaur	1.9	0.5 m units × average price £2.80

It is very rare that the company you are planning to buy operates solely in a UK market where it is possible to obtain 'clean' Companies House or other publicly available information, thus providing accurate sales information on each participant. Even if this is available it is rare for competitors to focus exclusively on the target market and to have no other activity which confuses the picture. Inevitably some assumptions will have to be made.

COMMERCIAL RATIOS

Some of the main information sources for assumptions are set out below.

Sales per employee ratio

Where nothing else is available, sales per employee ratios are useful. But they can be dangerously misleading as:

- the products made or services offered by various suppliers are not often strictly comparable – some companies add more value than others;
- the product mix within a business can distort the result dramatically;

- employee numbers can be misleading: staff may be part-time or departments may have been outsourced while employee estimates provided to you may simply be wrong.

Despite the dangers set out above, anyone analysing an industry should have at least an idea of the range of employee/sales ratios in that industry.

Product value ratios

If you know how many products a company makes in a week, month or year and if you know the average value of the product, multiplying one by the other can provide a turnover estimate.

Product value ratios are useful in the absence of any other information. They can also be as dangerous as employee ratios. Pitfalls include the following:

- Few companies make a single homogeneous product.

- It is often difficult to obtain a high-quality estimate of the number of products made or sold.

- Service or spares revenues and income from other non-core activities can distort the picture substantially.

- Part or all of the product may be made in other plants or in other countries.

- Levels of investment and productivity can vary widely – car plants make between 30 and 120 cars per employee per annum.

Occasionally corollary suppliers can provide the key to product numbers. For example, the number of insulators sold for high-tension electricity transmission lines is a ratio of the number of pylons sold. Find out the number of pylons and the market for insulators starts to become clear. But this calculation is valid for new lines; it takes no account of the market for replacing old insulators. To work that out you would need to estimate the product life and arrive at an annual replacement ratio.

Equally if you ask a lollipop company how many wooden sticks it buys you will soon have a good estimate of how many lollipops it sells. You will have to question whether you have been given an accurate answer, be satisfied that the company is not stockpiling sticks, determine whether the sticks are delivered cut to length and that there is little stick wastage.

Capital equipment can also lead to useful ratios. In the carpet industry a manufacturer with three looms will not be making the same volume of carpets as a manufacturer with 30, whatever the age and relative productivity of the looms. If you can find out how much raw material each carpet manufacturer buys this can also lead to some useful ratios.

Other ratios

Each industry has other ratios which can be used. Examples of such ratios include the ratio of:

- activity to economic growth/unemployment/sector performance;
- product or service sold as a function of user or geographic market segments;
- new versus replacement sales;
- consumables/services items to product (e.g. cartridges to ink-jet printers).

COMBINING SOURCES

Anyone using assumptions based on ratios should be nervous of their validity. Ratios need to be verified by testing them on similar companies or markets. It is best to assume that they are wrong until they are proven right.

When it is possible to use two or more separate assumptions and arrive at corresponding results the person using them can start to feel comfortable. It is rarely possible to analyse a company or a market from too many angles.

Stating the information source

It is best to provide information sources because it allows:

- others to understand the basis for each assumption;
- scope for updating.

The source gives an indication of the quality of the estimate. In the example given in Table 5.1 Alphatool's sales estimate depends on the accuracy of two inputs: first, Companies House information which is pretty good, at least compared to many other sources; and second, a trade press interview with Alphatool's managing director in which he stated that half of his sales are in left-handed widgets, which is reasonably reliable.

Betaway's estimate is based on one-year-old Companies House information – it requires only that the company has performed in line with the market.

The information source for Calypso was an employee/sales ratio and for Dinosaur it was a product value ratio. These are less reliable, but a lot better than nothing. If further information comes to light later on either of these two companies, the information can be updated. The person updating the analysis will be thankful that the information sources were stated.

Market quantification
– an example

INTRODUCTION

This example has been chosen as it covers a market which everyone has heard of, but it is a market on which there is no published data. There are no public companies operating in the competition rowing boat market and it is not covered by commercial databases or market reports.

THE UK MARKET FOR COMPETITION ROWING BOATS

As part of the market element of a commercial due diligence programme, you have been asked to quantify the size of the market for competition rowing boats, as used in the University Boat Race.

To someone who knows little of this sector the task may appear difficult. In reality it is not. The steps and results in the following example show how an uninformed outsider might be able to conduct a detailed commercial evaluation of the sector.

Data collection

In this example it is assumed that the behaviour of market participants is similar to most markets:

- The competing rowing boat manufacturers are reluctant to share detailed information; they may sense that you are a potential competitor.

- Users are willing to share information, although they very rarely have a clear view of the market size.

- Suppliers to the competition rowing boat sector are a good source of information as they know the market they supply well and they sense that an organisation reviewing a market may eventually become a customer.

Table 6.1 sets out the steps taken to collect data and their outcomes.

Table 6.1 Preparatory data collection

Step	Result
■ Telephone Oxford or Cambridge University and ask to speak to someone who knows about rowing – you are put through to various boat club members and boathouse men	Informed of: ■ Amateur Rowing Association ■ *Rowing* magazine ■ Amerson boat-builders ■ Pinter boat and oar-makers ■ Erdmann, the world-leading German boat-builder
■ Telephone Amateur Rowing Association	Sent list of 150 rowing clubs and list of regattas
■ Telephone *Rowing* magazine	Sent back copies, informed of other boat-builders and their suppliers. Contact happy to assist further at a later stage
Desk research	
■ Contact Companies House for financial data	Reports arrive on two of the boat-builders
■ Interrogate import/export statistics	Discover that data is combined with many other boat types
■ Conduct on-line searches through commercial databases	Very little useful information arises
Data collection	
■ Telephone boat-builders to ask for brochures and prices; make other enquiries about boats made and staff numbers if possible	Some useful data is collected (*see* Table 6.2, Page 64)
■ Telephone a sample of rowing clubs to ask how many boats on average they purchase per annum	Indicative of answer – clubs 2 p.a.; colleges 3 p.a. One sends you price lists
■ Telephone oar manufacturers to ask how many oars are made each year	Indicative answer: UK market is 5000 p.a.
■ Telephone suppliers to boat-makers to establish how many units of riggers, sliding seats, speaker systems, etc. are supplied to boat-builders	Hard data obtained from some; indicative data from others

Analysis

The data collection process has developed a patchwork of information. An analytical approach must now be used to quantify the competition rowing boat market.

- For one company we have obtained its sales level from Companies House and employee numbers from reading its brochure. Work out a turnover/employee ratio which can be used as a rough benchmark for other boat-makers.

- Create an analytical framework for the market and decide on the segmentation. It will be by:
  - boat type – eight, four, pair and single;
  - boat-maker;
  - user segment – universities, clubs and export.

- We know how many oars are sold in the UK; establish how many are sold with new boats and how many just replace old oars. Work out the total of oars sold with new boats (of all types).

- From the number of speaker systems sold apply a ratio for boats sold with speakers, deduct an estimated amount for the replacement and retrofit markets and estimate the number of 'eights' sold.

- From estimates made by outrigger suppliers make another attempt at estimating the number of boats sold.

The data developed is leading to a possible quantification of the UK market, cross referenced from a number of sources. The ultimate goal will now be to establish the sizes of competitors.

- Set out the competitors in a table with the known data. For example, for some companies the number of boats made or the total value of sales are known; for others you have employee numbers or quantities of outriggers purchased (*see* Tables 6.2 and 6.3).

- Make whatever other assumptions are possible with the corresponding data. For example, we know that Amerson buys 320 outriggers. Given an average of four per boat that means Amerson makes 80 boats per annum. Cross-reference this assumption to any others made possible through ratios such as employee/sales.

- Make other assumptions and add them to the picture. Of the 5000 oars sold, 30 per cent are exported and 20 per cent are replacements. Oar manufacturers count the two oars required for a single (person) boat as one unit in their calculations. Consequently 2500 oars are sold with new boats. On average five are sold per boat – the average boat size is a 'four' and this includes one spare oar per boat and the assumption that all new boats have new oars purchased in the same year is reasonable. Therefore the boat market is 500 per annum.

- The process continues with further data collection – on defining issues. For example, if the turnover/employee or outrigger/boat ratios appear robust, this data should be sought and applied to each manufacturer as it will allow us to finalise the market size.

- Allocate the possible boat sales by manufacturers – but use italics for those figures which are no more than guesses and list all of your assumptions.
- Cross-reference the data to arrive at a turnover figure for each manufacturer. Add them up to obtain a market size figure.

Conclusion

Tables 6.2 and 6.3 show the data gathered from the preliminary investigations and Table 6.4 shows the outcome from this market quantification.

Table 6.2 Data collected from desk research and initial enquiries

	Company data			Boats made				Total boats	Value of boats (£000)
	Employees	Outriggers	Speakers	Eights	Fours	Pairs	Singles		
Amerson		320							
Pinter	30								1800
Erdmann			40	25		0	0		
Regatta	15				30				
Other									
Total								500*	

Assumptions are in italics.
*Based on oar market calculation.

Table 6.3 Development of data

Ratios developed		Average boat values	
Employee : sales	£60 000	Eight	£13 000
Outriggers : boats	4	Four	£10 000
Speakers : eights	1	Pair	£7 000
Speakers : fours	0.25	Single	£4 000

Table 6.4 Data enhanced by application of assumptions

	Company data			Boats made				Total boats	Value of boats (£000)
	Employees	Outriggers	Speakers	Eights	Fours	Pairs	Singles		
Amerson	13	320		25	30	20	5	80	800*
Pinter	30			50	90	25	20	185	1800*
Erdmann			40	25	60	0	0	85	925
Regatta	15			30	30	20	10	90	900*
Other					10	10	45	65**	350
Total								500	4775

*   Note that turnover estimates are not entirely consistent with boat numbers multiplied by average boat price.
** Size of other segment calculated by subtracting boat volumes of all major players from the total boat market.

This example shows how it is possible to build a reasonable view of a market size from outside the market. It also shows the imperfections of any such market quantification, but also how you can use a series of assumptions and intelligent guesswork to arrive at a concrete result.

Should it be particularly important to obtain a more precise market quantification, more interviews could be conducted and more data sought. The quality of data required for a market quantification is always a function of the extent of risk. If you are about to enter the market by acquiring a boat-builder, at least this level of analysis would be required. If a paint manufacturer is considering the launch of a branded paint for this market segment, the level of detail in this example would be excessive.

In reality these methods normally provide at least an adequate understanding of the size of a market. In cases where the data are weak the person or organisation presenting it should be frank and always allow for discussion or other inputs to improve the data or the analysis.

Obviously, market quantifications should be as accurate as possible. However, understanding trends and factors driving profitability within the market can be even more important than the market size itself. It is less relevant to know that a market is worth £90m or £110m than to know that in five years' time all the competitors will have had their margins halved due to intensifying competition.

Therefore having quantified and understood the market, a CDD investigation should go on to consider market trends and then the competitive position of each player in the market. In particular it must assess the performance of the acquisition target against the rest of the market.

MARKET TRENDS – AN EXAMPLE

Now that the quantification of the competition rowing boat market is complete we need to examine the second key commercial ingredient to market attractiveness: market trend information.

The central question which a new entrant should pose is: 'Are there favourable trends for profitability?'

Some of the factors influencing profitability are set out in Table 6.5.

Table 6.5 Factors influencing profitability

Factor	Impact
■ Market growth	Positive
■ Consolidation	Positive for major players
■ New entrants	Negative
■ Concentration of purchasing power	Negative
■ Rapid technical change	Positive for major players
■ Growth of rival technologies	Negative
■ Vertical or horizontal integration of suppliers	Negative

The UK market for competition rowing boats – market trends

Here are some of the questions which you may address in our example.

Market growth

■ Have the boat-builders expanded or contracted?

■ Have related companies and other suppliers such as oar and outrigger manufacturers expanded or contracted?

■ Is the market base changing – are there more or less:

– rowing clubs and college boat clubs?

– members of the Amateur Rowing Association?

– readers of *Rowing* magazine?

■ Is rowing growing internationally?

Consolidation

■ How has the number of boat-builders changed over the past five years (including bankruptcies, takeovers and new entrants)?

- Have the market shares of the leading players grown significantly over the past five years?

New entrants

- Which boat-builders have entered (successfully or not) the market over the past five years?

Concentration of purchasing power

- Do rowing clubs and college boat clubs purchase autonomously?
- Do universities purchase co-operatively?
- Are clubs merging?

Rapid technical change

- What are the current technical changes (e.g. new plastics, hull design)?
- Do these changes accelerate obsolescence, shortening the replacement cycle?

Growth of rival technologies

- Is there a threat of a new technology superseding current industry norms (e.g. in the way that plastic replaced wood in the 1980s)?

Integration

- Might an oar-maker make boats and offer a combined package?

Conclusion

An analysis of these trends will allow you to assess how the attractiveness of the market will evolve. You should also then compare the current position of the acquisition target and its resources to the major trends. This analysis will allow you to determine its competitive position.

Conducting analysis

Once you have collected all the information you need and plugged the information gaps you can get on with the analysis.

WHAT IS ANALYSIS?

Analysis is the process of interpreting data and information so that you can reach a set of conclusions.

Analysis is based on:

- taking the information available;
- making a series of simple comparisons;
- drawing conclusions.

There are three keys to success for anyone conducting analysis. They must:

- establish the issues critical in the market or to the company under review:

  'are we just re-arranging the deck chairs on the Titanic?'

- select information which is relevant and valid:

  'garbage in, garbage out.'

- present comparable information on each of them:

  'compare apples to apples.'

WORKING OUT WHAT MATTERS

Some issues are important to all companies and markets. At the risk of stating the obvious these include:

- profit levels
- market size
- growth rate.

The relative importance of many other issues such as the number of competitors, fragmentation of customers, technology requirements and the importance of price as a purchasing criterion will vary according to the market. Their importance will also vary according to the agenda of the organisation planning the acquisition.

For example, a low cost base niche player in IT consultancy may be attracted to a market dominated by major players, such as Andersen Consulting, if it can find a way to differentiate its product, perhaps through price or service. Therefore this niche player may wish to acquire another specialist in a related niche which can also compete with the likes of Andersen Consulting. The two firms would benefit from some economies of scale but would remain differentiated. A major consultancy would be unwise to try to grow in this market through the acquisition of a niche player unless it could prove that the combined business would significantly improve competitiveness, possibly to the extent of rivalling the market leader.

Also:

As in the classic razor and blade example, ink-jet printer manufacturers profit highly from selling replacement ink cartridges, but only when there is sufficient demand for their consumables and their volumes reach critical mass. However, once they have surpassed critical mass they must then change the design sufficiently often to deter other consumables makers from copying or refilling their cartridges.

Also:

In the early and mid-1990s some holiday tour operators profited from high interest rates; others focused on operational efficiencies. A sharp decline in interest rates will impact on one type of tour operator more than on another. Two rival tour operators may have very similar bottom lines, but depending on the chosen business model an acquirer or an investor would find one more attractive than the other.

Each of these examples demonstrates the importance of understanding the fundamental issues which drive the growth and profitability of markets and individual businesses in those markets.

CRITICAL SUCCESS FACTORS

To avoid wasting time and energy perusing relatively unimportant issues you should establish the critical success factors (CSFs) in a market.

There is no fixed rule as to how many CSFs apply to any particular business; as a guide there are often between four and eight. Always start with a clean sheet of paper.

Critical success factors vary from one segment to another. For example, a transport company analysing the private house-moving market and the corporate house-moving market (where the move is paid for by the employer) will find the differences listed in Table 7.1.

Table 7.1 Critical success factors for removals companies by market segment

Factor	Private segment	Corporate segment
Price	Low bidder wins	Appearance of competitiveness suffices
Delivery	Can be late	On-time delivery is essential
No losses of items	Best avoided	Essential (don't lose the MD's heirlooms)
Brand	Useful	Essential to give confidence
International network	Nice to have	Coverage is essential wherever managers are sent

Once you have established the critical success factors for a business a very useful analysis can be based on a review of the capabilities of competing suppliers. A new entrant can match its skills to each critical success factor. It can then assess the cost and likelihood of being able to match the requirements of the market.

In the above example, a transport company seeking entry to the corporate removals market can take its current and potential resource base, match it against the issues identified as important – price, delivery, no losses, brand and network – and assess the difficulty of adapting its skills. Few would succeed.

A small haulage firm would find domestic removals more suited to its skills; an international freight forwarder would be better suited to the corporate market. The decision will of course also be determined by a wide range of other issues such as the acquisition candidate's financial strength, human resources and the level of customer overlap between the two markets. In both cases market entry through organic growth should be considered as an alternative.

If the international freight forwarder is determined to enter the corporate market and its current skills are a poor fit then acquisition becomes appropriate. The skills and resources of potential acquisition targets can be compared to the industry CSFs.

ANALYTICAL METHODS AND TOOLS

There is a wide range of analytical tools at the disposal of anyone conducting a CDD programme. Essentially these tools allow you to make comparisons. If you are not used to analytical tools do not be blinded by their supposed science. In many cases you need only apply one or two of the simplest tools to analyse a market. If in doubt keep the analysis simple.

Trend chart

AMR International has developed a trend chart to assess a company's performance against the critical success factors in an industry. It is simple to use. First establish the critical success factors in the sector, then use a series of arrows to map the company's performance over time relative to each CSF (see Figure 7.1). The arrows must flow forming a continuous line.

Fig. 7.1 AMR trend chart – corporate removals acquisition candidate mapped against CSFs

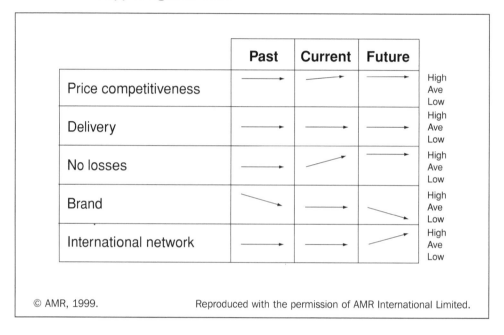

© AMR, 1999.   Reproduced with the permission of AMR International Limited.

Although all of the data in the trend chart is qualitative it has the distinct advantage of allowing the reader to see how the business is performing and to assess its prospects. After all, an acquirer is paying today for tomorrow's profits.

A glance down the right-hand column shows how the company will perform in the future.

Market share analysis

Precise market share data is not always important. More important are market drivers and their impact on the relative market share of the target and on its profitability.

The example below shows why. In this example Acquirer A and Acquirer B are considering the same acquisition. Both have assessed market size and growth, but they have reached different conclusions. The impact of these conclusions is set out in Tables 7.2 and 7.3.

Table 7.2 Impact of market analysis on an acquisition target's profitability – (1)

	Analysis of Acquirer A	Reality	Analysis of Acquirer B
Target's current year profits*	£10 m	£10 m	£10 m
Market size**	£1000 m	£1500 m	£2000 m
Market growth**	+10%	+15%	+20%
Market share trend	Stable	Stable	Stable
Margin trend	Stable	Stable	Stable
Following year's profits	£11 m	£11.5 m	£12 m

* Provided by seller

** Estimates by the acquirers

Table 7.3 Impact of market analysis on an acquisition target's profitability – (2)

	Analysis of Acquirer A	Reality	Analysis of Acquirer B
Target's current year profits*	£10 m	£10 m	£10 m
Market size**	£1000 m	£1500 m	£2000 m
Market growth**	+10%	+15%	+20%
Market share trend	Stable	Stable	+10%
Margin trend	Stable	Stable	+10%
Following year's profits***	£11 m	£11.5 m	£14 m

* Provided by seller

** Estimates by the acquirers

*** Margins are 10%

The market size and share analyses of Acquirers A and B vary wildly – one is twice the other. But so long as the target is not hitting the limit of its potential market share, the question of market size is irrelevant. The factors driving future profitability are market growth, the sustainability of the target's market share and the mix of other factors impacting on profitability. In Table 7.2, the £1 m difference in future profitability estimates is attributed to Acquirer B's higher growth estimate.

Table 7.3 shows how more bullish estimates of Acquirer B in the areas of market share trend and margin trend further impact on profitability.

Acquirer B now forecasts profits at £14 m, £3 m ahead of Acquirer A in the first year of ownership. Acquirer B is much more optimistic about market share trend and margin trend. It looks like it is talking itself into the acquisition. It will need strong evidence from its CDD investigations that these projections are plausible.

These calculations are only on a stand-alone basis and no integration benefits have been taken into consideration.

If both acquirers were planning to pay a multiple of 10 times profits to acquire the business Acquirer B would be planning to pay £140m, £30m more than Acquirer A.

SWOT analysis

A SWOT is an excellent single-page analysis of a company. Any commercial due diligence report should have a SWOT analysis linked to its conclusions page.

A well structured SWOT based on sound research provides a clear view of a company. It also indicates the areas where actions are required to sustain performance and to grow the business. A SWOT focuses in particular on two areas of CDD analysis: competitive position and management.

Guidelines for the issues which should be addressed in each element of a SWOT are set out in Figure 7.2.

Figure 7.3 sets out a worked example based on the rowing boat example detailed in Chapter 6.

Fig. 7.2 SWOT analysis

Strengths	Weaknesses
Current product, brand, distribution, pricing, management or other strengths of the business. These strengths generate profits now and should also do so in the future.	Current weaknesses of the business. These weaknesses can often be overcome, but at a cost through management action or investment. Often the opportunities will include ways of countering these weaknesses.
Opportunities	**Threats**
Areas of growth or opportunities for future growth, given suitable management action or investment.	Issues beyond the control of the company which could damage its position and performance. It is important to assess the scale of these threats and the likelihood of them occurring. It is also important to consider what actions can be taken to mitigate the impact of threats.

Fig. 7.3   Example SWOT: Amerson Boat Builders

Strengths	Weaknesses
• Brand *Rowing magazine reports Amerson to be the leading UK brand* • Competitive price position *Evident from price lists, backed up by users* • UK rowing team endorsement *The only UK boat-builder used by UK teams in competitions (most boats used are Erdmann)*	• Inconsistent product quality *Two experienced boathouse men report inconsistent quality, particularly faulty shoulders* • Delivery time *Numerous buyers complain of late delivery* • Administration *Some buyers complain of lost correspondence and mis-invoicing*
Opportunities	**Threats**
• Benefit from market growth *Rowing magazine forecasts continued growth, particularly given the UK team's Olympic success* • Develop export market *Less well established rivals have developed export sales* • Acquire outrigger company *Economies of scale and joint technical development may be achievable* • Develop maintenance package *Smaller clubs would be interested in an annual maintenance package*	• Reduced university budgets *University budget pressure is impacting boat clubs' purchasing* • Erdmann developing UK market *The world-renowned German boat-builder is rumoured to be setting up a UK sales office*

Although SWOT analysis may be considered by some members of the business community to be old-fashioned, it remains very useful and is particularly well suited to CDD. Make sure you think through the issues carefully. The SWOT should highlight all of the significant issues and it can be used to draw a conclusion, such as 'the threats outweigh the opportunities – do not buy the company'.

Attractiveness of market/ability to compete

Frequently discussions about a company's prospects or market entry can be distilled down to two key questions:

■ Is this an attractive market (or market segment) to be in?

■ How well can (or could) we compete in it?

These questions can be addressed through the basic attractiveness of market/ability to compete matrix set out in Figure 7.4.

Fig. 7.4 Attractiveness of market/ability to compete matrix

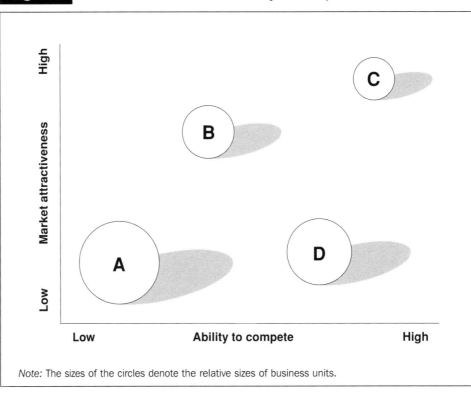

Note: The sizes of the circles denote the relative sizes of business units.

Figure 7.4 analyses an acquisition target; A, B, C and D are its four business units, each operating in a different market. This group is not an attractive target. Its largest business unit is in an unattractive market and it is relatively uncompetitive.

So, how can you combine the information you have gathered on the target and its market to compile a market attractiveness/ability to compete matrix?

Preparing data for the market

Data for the market attractiveness axis is prepared by combining the two key issues – size and trends. Figure 7.5 sets out how this is done.

Depending on the level of detail required, a subjective or a quantitative answer can suffice. If a quantitative answer is required, you can follow a simple scoring method:

Relative profit levels of participants	0 – 5
Favourable market trends	0 – 5
Market attractiveness	0 – 10

The largest markets with the most favourable trends have ten points; small declining markets will score zero.

In rapidly developing markets, a current analysis can be misleading: it may be more useful to estimate market attractiveness at the end of a two-year period.

Fig. 7.5 Market attractiveness

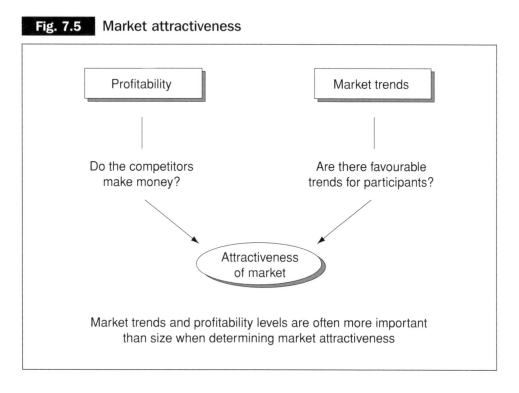

Fig. 7.6 Ability to compete

Data for the ability to compete axis is prepared by comparing available skills and resources to the demands of the market on its participants. Figure 7.6 sets out the issues.

Fig. 7.6 Ability to compete

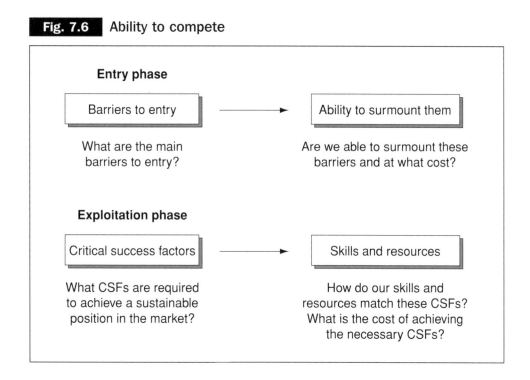

As with market attractiveness, a subjective view can often suffice to position a company's competitiveness along the ability to compete axis.

Should a quantitative result be required then the relative costs of overcoming barriers to entry and of matching the industry's critical success factors can be assessed. These costs can then be plotted on the ability to compete axis.

As shown in the example in Figure 7.4, a glance at the outcome can bring you to a quick conclusion. Figure 7.7 sets out a more detailed analysis of the types of management approach which should be adopted in the various areas of the market attractiveness/ability to compete matrix.

Fig. 7.7 Market attractiveness/ability to compete management actions

	Weak	Medium	Strong
High	**Build selectively** • Invest to grow at maximum digestible rate • Concentrate effort on maintaining strength	**Invest to build** • Challenge for leadership • Build selectively on strengths • Reinforce vulnerable areas	**Protect** • Defend strengths • Concentrate on attractive segments • Manage for current earnings
Medium	**Limited development** • Look for ways to expand without high risk; otherwise minimise investment and rationalise operations	**Selective** • Protect existing programme • Concentrate investments in segments where profitability is good and risk is relatively low	**Build** • Invest heavily in most attractive segments • Emphasise profitability by raising productivity
Low	**Divest** • Sell at time that will maximise cash value • Cut fixed costs and avoid investment meanwhile	**Manage for profit** • Protect position in most profitable segments • Upgrade product line • Minimise investment	**Protect and build** • Specialise around limited strengths • Seek ways to overcome weaknesses • Withdraw if indications of sustainable growth are lacking

Market attractiveness (vertical axis)

Ability to compete (horizontal axis: Weak, Medium, Strong)

Perceptual maps

Perceptual maps are an excellent way of providing a market overview with an indication of competitive position.

For example, a perceptual map with sales on one axis and on the other quality of technology (a CSF) is set out in Figure 7.8.

Fig. 7.8 Relative performance of competitors

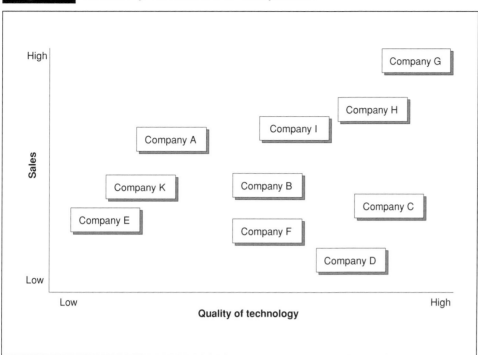

MAKING YOUR OWN TOOLS

Most analysis is no more than the comparison of two data sets on opposing axes.

There are no fixed rules about which two sets of data should be compared. An experienced business development manager or consultant will try a series of comparisons and select those that are the most meaningful.

On the other hand, financial evaluation is closer to being a science; a well known set of measures such as margin and return on capital can provide meaningful comparisons. Some companies such as GEC and BTR became famous for managing their businesses by ratios. Hanson became famous for selecting acquisition targets through financial ratios alone.

The art of commercial evaluation for CDD lies in selecting the two sets of data or issues to put on the axes of your otherwise blank piece of paper. Some of the data sets (hard comparisons) or issues (soft comparisons) which can be used are set out in Table 7.4.

Table 7.4 Comparative data and issues

Data	Issues
Sales	Image
Profits	Customer satisfaction
Growth	Culture
Employee numbers	Management skills
Market share	Ability to invest
Number of sites/other key assets	Quality
Ownership (public/private)	Market coverage
Technology (digital/analogue, etc.)	Critical success factors (industry-specific)
Scope of sales/distribution	
Number of products in range	

Table 7.4 is not intended to be exhaustive. It does not include industry-specific measures such as the number of beds per hotel in the hotel industry, numbers of subscribers in mobile telecoms and hundreds of others. Critical success factors are often relevant issues.

Draw perceptual maps comparing various data and issues – see what you come up with!

PRESENTATION OF ANALYSIS

Any manager with a PC can now make a beautiful presentation. However, charting data does not make it any more accurate or make the comparisons any more valid. The key is to have accurate information and to compare the issues which matter in the market and to the company.

The basic rules of presenting analysis are as follows:

■ First work out what should be analysed, and then present it.

■ Do not communicate too many messages on a single page.

■ Provide enough information and sufficient clarification on the page for the recipient to understand it.

■ Always use consistent data for comparisons.

■ If one issue is being compared to another on a series of charts – say, for the transport company example earlier in the chapter, price versus international network and price versus number of lost heirlooms – always chart price on the same axis.

Analytical tools can be adapted to suit a market; it is not necessary to stick religiously to the precise structure of a tool.

Reporting

TIMETABLE

As time is inevitably in short supply you should set a reporting timetable, and adhere to it. Build in the other elements of the due diligence investigation and make sure that you have allowed some time for their results to be co-ordinated. You should also schedule interim checkpoints and feedback sessions, even if they are only by telephone conference.

Be realistic about what can be achieved within the acquisition timetable. If the timetable is extended use this to the advantage of the due diligence team and obtain any detail on key issues which time constraints forced you to pass over.

METHODS AND STYLES

Information can be delivered in many different ways, with varying levels of presentational skill. In fact the reporting method and style are not all that important; what matters is whether the content is well organised and whether the findings are based on sound information and analysis. Beautiful charts and graphs can improve presentations, but they must be legible and the data readable. Some 3D charts are very difficult to read.

THE REPORT

Presentation meeting

If consultants are being used they should present the findings of their work. This allows more value to be obtained as the consultants can be questioned on their reasoning, further information and insights may surface and scenarios can be jointly developed during the meeting.

Equally an internal team is best asked to present its findings – this encourages the team to make an extra effort while organising its findings.

Written report

A written report should be provided. It should include:

- terms of reference
- conclusions
- analysis

- key data

- interview notes and other supporting information.

It is worth re-emphasising the key topics which must be included in the conclusions. They are:

- executive summary;

- SWOT of the target;

- trend chart mapping the target against industry CSFs;

- market issues:
  - growth
  - structure
  - trends for profitability;

- competitive position:
  - ability to compete
  - capability vs CSFs;

- management skills and resource gaps:
  - key managers
  - weaknesses;

- integration action list;

- buy/don't buy decision.

Interim reporting

Interim reports are very useful. Even if time constraints do not allow for an interim report or meeting, it is best to hold a conference call and discuss the key issues. This allows everyone involved to focus their thinking. The direction for the second half can be set and, hopefully, the CDD team can then satisfy its brief.

However, interim reports can be dangerous. If consultants are being used they will have conducted about half of their work, but they may have only one-third of their results. Consultants may appear to be coming up with wishy-washy results at this stage, which can lead to nervousness about the quality of the final results. Also the consultants are unlikely to provide very negative interim findings for a number of reasons. These include:

- they may not be entirely sure of their ground and will still be developing their arguments;

- they are unlikely to take a position from which it would be embarrassing to climb down at the final reporting stage;

■ they would be loath to make the results entirely negative as this may lead to their work being curtailed and their fee reduced.

Whatever the negatives and time pressures, interim reporting is useful. Overall, the more contact between client, consultant and other members of the due diligence team, the better the end result is likely to be.

REPORTING AND THE TARGET

As the CDD report can have a fundamental impact on the deal, a well managed acquisition candidate will be inquisitive about the content of the report, or it may well try to influence its content. The report is clearly for the acquirer's use; it should be written for the acquirer, with sensitive pages removed from any copies which may be provided to the seller. After the deal is concluded the report should provide useful integration insights for the combined businesses.

In cases where the results are negative the report, or a presentation by consultants if they have been used, can be a very powerful weapon in the negotiations. This topic is covered in greater detail in the next chapter.

Many of these issues relate to consultants. Nonetheless managers who are conducting a commercial due diligence programme with internal resources will find many of these points equally relevant.

9

Using the output

THE ACQUISITION DECISION

The primary purpose of the CDD investigation is to decide whether or not to buy the company. If the CDD team is heading towards a negative decision it must communicate with the acquisition decision makers in the purchasing company well in advance. The project director can then ensure that all the necessary angles have been covered, plan how the decision can be taken and how it will be communicated to the target.

VALUATION

One of the key outcomes of the commercial due diligence programme will be the analysis of the major factors impacting on the future profitability of the acquisition candidate. These should be fed into the valuation. The level of useful detail can go far beyond just including a view on market trends. If a discounted cash flow (DCF) analysis is being used the business should be broken down by activity or even product line; the results of interviews can then be used to validate sales and profit projections by product line.

> For example, CDD on a market-leading British engineer supplying the original equipment manufacturers (OEMs) of white goods found that US customers were planning production increases above those already declared to the target. But in Europe customers were indifferent to the target as a supplier and competitors were planning major product launches. The DCFs being used to value the acquisition candidate were adjusted positively for the US and negatively for Europe, reducing the company's value by 25 per cent. The seller was shown why the valuation had changed and how the new figure has been reached. It had no scope for argument.

As the major accounting-based firms are highly concerned by possible litigation they are loath to make their own forecasts. Consequently they are delighted to latch on to an external validation of their forecasts from a CDD specialist. As stated earlier, valuation is largely a function of future profitability.

NEGOTIATION

The due diligence findings are an excellent negotiating tool, principally on price but also on terms and deal structure. For example, the buyer can use negative findings about customer satisfaction in a particular market segment or on the declining competitive position of a business unit to negotiate the price down. The buyer can attribute a lower, or even a nil, value to these parts of the business.

> For example, a British specialist recruitment agency had agreed to sell itself to a US giant. The British company had excellent profitability and was beating its targets. As a part of ISO 9000 it carried out a quarterly customer satisfaction audit which showed few customer complaints. However, commercial due diligence unearthed substantial customer dissatisfaction due to weak account management and a series of staff walkouts, some founding new competitors.
>
> The results came as a shock to the seller. The bad news was presented to the seller in a carefully structured presentation. The ensuing negotiations resulted in a $10m reduction in the acquisition price and a revised deal structure.

Some vendors try to limit the scope for negotiation before the due diligence programme starts by fixing the price and making it clear to the buyer that they will not budge. Whatever the other side's negotiating tactics may be, the buyer needs to conduct a thorough valuation to prove the value of the business and to assess the areas of risk.

On some occasions major commercial issues can become the subject of delayed payments or the purchaser can seek protection through warranties and indemnities. For example, if the renewal of a key contract will impact significantly on value then part of the payment can be withheld until it is renewed.

PREPARING THE INTEGRATION PLAN

The value of using commercial due diligence in integration planning has only recently been fully realised by many acquirers.

Those companies which plan integration in advance tend to be the most successful acquirers. Williams plc is famous for acting at dawn by sending a post-acquisition integration team into the acquired company and implementing change rapidly. Studies such as the AMR/ICME survey (*see* D. Rankine (1997) *A Practical Guide to Acquisition*, Wiley) show that where management is seconded rapidly there is a better post-acquisition atmosphere and that the financial targets of the acquired company are more likely to be met.

Preparing the integration plan in advance also increases the chances of success in another way. Those acquirers which have not prepared integration plans in at least some level of detail cannot have valued the business accurately. Valuation depends first on the stand-alone performance of the target and then on the 'synergies' brought by the acquirer. In order to work out the synergies – which can be positive as well as negative – an integration plan needs to have been developed.

> For example, a leading player in the Scandinavian travel industry presented itself for sale to a UK buyer claiming healthy growth projections and emphasising the skills and track record of its high-profile chairman. CDD showed that the interference of the chairman had been negative, the company's position in Sweden had been damaged by misjudged pricing and that its two Finnish operations were unintegrated and Finnish management were at loggerheads.
>
> All of these points were used to negotiate the price, but more to plan integration. Overall CDD also revealed possible cost-savings in the region of £10m; these were put at the top of the integration priorities.

The full integration plan will include a wide range of issues, those covered by a CDD programme being just a part. Table 9.1 sets out those integration issues which can be informed by the CDD process.

Table 9.1 Example CDD inputs to integration

Product
- product and service weaknesses which need to be enhanced to maintain or improve competitive advantage
- positioning of product offerings

Distribution
- integration, or not, of distribution channels
- feasibility of selling through each other's channels

Sales and marketing
- method of communicating ownership change to customers
- preservation of brand, brand positioning
- co-ordination of sales efforts between acquirer and the acquired company

Price positioning
- opportunities for price adjustments

Business development
- product and service enhancement
- new product or service launches
- new market entry opportunities

Management
- key team members who must be motivated and retained
- weak areas, as witnessed by underperforming areas of the business
- skills which can be transferred to the acquirer
- desirability, or not, of cultural convergence

These inputs to integration are based largely on an analysis of information gathered through interviews in the market. The process is also informed through the CDD team's meetings with management and its understanding of the acquirer's operations. The CDD inputs to integration are more pertinent to business development issues than to cost-cutting opportunities.

10

Examples of CDD outcomes

Tables 10.1 to 10.3 set out examples of CDD programmes in which the commercial due diligence revealed significant issues which affected the acquisition decision, the price paid or the integration planning. The examples are set out by the three cornerstone categories of CDD: market, competitive position and management.

Table 10.1 CDD outcome: market

Sector	Issue	How it was revealed	Impact
Consumer electronics accessory	Inexperienced management's claims of explosive growth with unproven product were borne out	Trade buyers	Acquisition justified
Temporary buildings	Overstretched market leader forced to discount heavily to maintain volumes	Competitors, suppliers, customers	Acquisition and market entry abandoned
Soft drinks	German market being served through grey imports to avoid the troublesome local distributor	Local importers	Acquisition justified as demand in new high-margin market was proven

Table 10.2 CDD outcome: competitive position

Sector	Issue	How it was revealed	Impact
Medical	Vertical integration by a massive near competitor changed the agenda of key suppliers and restricted the target's route to market	Near competitor	Issue used in negotiations with vendor to restrict price
Engineering	Competitor's parent company was set to invest heavily in new product development	Competitor	Acquisition halted
Recruitment agency	Strong financial performance belied weakening customer relations and impending termination of accounts	Customers	Price renegotiated; earn-out introduced
Instrumentation	Product performance questioned by leading experts, thus unsettling current and potential customers	Industry experts and academics	Acquisition abandoned
Electronics	Indecisive management had lost customer focus of an otherwise strong company	Customers and former employees	Offer to pay premium price withdrawn; lower offer made
Electronics	Customer loyalty seriously impacted by poor service record	Customers	Offer reduced

Table 10.3 CDD outcome: management

Sector	Issue	How it was revealed	Impact
Electronics	The entrepreneur founder feared that he had inherited heart disease and believed he would die at 45	Founder of largest competitor	Earn-out deal dropped
Business services	All staff with ambition had left a bureaucratic organisation which had failed to exploit its near-monopoly position	Former employees, customers and competitors	Offer reduced
Engineering	Indecisive management had lost the company's market leadership position as competitors outpaced it with new product launches	Competitors and customers	Offer withdrawn
Construction	Entrepreneurial owner's sales skills masked poor service and under-resourced management structure	Customers and competitors	Offer reduced
Business services	Management of the target by far the best in the industry	Customers and competitors	Managers incentivised, tied in and encouraged to spread best practice in the acquirer
Plastics	Eccentric octogenarian owner secured the best prices from both suppliers and customers	Suppliers and customers	Premium price justified; strong management hired to replace owner
Engineering	Boardroom transformed by appointment of new MD	Partner company	MD retained and encouraged to strengthen his team

The right team and project management

When a major acquisition is planned and the level of risk consequently is high, a commercial evaluation team should be assembled.

RESOURCES

An operational manager or business development executive can satisfactorily undertake a modest commercial evaluation of a business development initiative on his or her own. However, a one-person team cannot hope to deal with all of the complexities which anything but the smallest acquisition brings.

A small team will inevitably rely more heavily on internal information sources than on external sources as it will have neither the time nor the resources to conduct extensive enquiries outside the organisation. Starting with internal information sources and commercial databases is no bad thing. A well organised business development manager will have rapid access to the most relevant information sources for his sector and a network of useful contacts to call on.

Indeed organisations sometimes under-utilise the knowledge and experience of internal managers; you may even have a former employee of the target on your payroll.

The best way to approach a major due diligence programme is to call on extra resources and bring together a project team.

PROJECT TEAMS

Ideally, the overall due diligence team comprises a balance of disciplines.

Team composition

The overall due diligence team members should represent the disciplines relevant to the investigation; the team may comprise internal or external resources, or a mix of the two. Often the overall due diligence team will have representatives from:

- marketing or strategy
- finance
- technical or operational
- legal
- general management/human resources
- IT
- any other relevant disciplines.

There is no rule as to whether the team members should be internal or external. This decision will depend on the level and quality of internal resource available, the specific skills required and cost.

Team leader and project management

However the team is comprised, it is essential that the team has clear leadership and that the team leader is easily contactable. This is equally true of single or multi-disciplinary teams.

The team leader will be responsible for ensuring that team members:

- communicate regularly and brief each other on developments;
- remain focused on the issues of commercial importance;
- follow up new angles as they arise;
- are sufficiently rigorous in their approach;
- stick to the timetable;
- liaise with the financial and legal teams as required;
- deliver results which are coherent with each other.

On major acquisition due diligence projects a highly effective approach is to hold regular review meetings. These meetings ensure excellent communication between team members and can get the best out of advisors, whose professional pride encourages them to outperform others on the team. While this approach leads to the best results, it can be expensive if the advisors around the table are all running 'taxi meters' as opposed to working on fixed-price contracts. It is even possible to get lawyers to agree to a fixed fee on some occasions.

> For example, in 1993 BET had finished reorganising itself and was considering its first major acquisition for over three years. Although the target, Style Conferences, was apparently well run, BET took no chances and set up a weekly due diligence team meeting. Thus when the commercial due diligence team revealed what appeared to be a rival start-up sponsored by the existing management the issue could be rapidly reviewed by other due diligence team members. The team leader then decided how to use this information in the negotiations.

If the weekly, or even more frequent, meeting approach is not taken, regular communication and co-ordination are essential.

The background of the team leader can be from any discipline. The ability to lead and to manage projects is more important than whether the individual is a strategist, a technical expert, an accountant or a lawyer.

INTERNAL SYSTEMS

Considerable information passes through the hands of managers. If correctly captured and organised, this knowledge can become invaluable when a company or market needs close scrutiny. However, it is not easy to make internal systems work effectively. Even when internal systems do work well they are more likely to provide a good starting point for CDD programmes rather than the result.

Systems are better than keeping information in managers' heads

Ideally competitor information should be captured in internal systems, as opposed to residing in the heads of top managers. It may be difficult to pin down the manager, and obviously when the manager leaves so does the information. A further problem is that, when asked, a knowledgeable manager will not always have the time, or the inclination, to dredge his or her memory for full details on that particular company.

The difficulty of systems

Internal competitor and market information systems tend to fail when they are too complex or time consuming. Other reasons for internal systems failing are simple lack of organisation or insufficient 'buy-in'.

Setting up and maintaining internal competitor and market information systems which can be used for CDD is very difficult. This is particularly so in medium or small-sized businesses.

> For example, an engineering contractor specialising in industrial control (SCADA) systems had the opportunity to acquire a competitor against which it often bid in tenders. But the acquirer had not set up a system to document its individual performance against competitors. Such an internal system would have immediately yielded data on the relative performance of the proposed acquisition target. The potential acquirer ended up paying outsiders to cover this ground during CDD.

The reasons for internal systems failing are insufficient motivation and incentives to:

- set them up;
- maintain them;
- use the results.

103

Large organisations such as retail chains and oil companies are typically better organised in their approach than smaller companies. In these large firms the business development or planning department can champion and manage the system. The output is seen as useful as it is often integrated with other systems.

Procedures to formalise

Many companies can put themselves at an advantage over competitors by improving their basic procedures. Some useful examples include:

- filing and collating press clippings on competitors, as opposed to throwing them out with the newspaper or trade journal;
- holding on to all promotional material of competitors, including their internal newsletters;
- monitoring competitor websites on a regular basis;
- making up contact reports on competitors;
- documenting job interviews with employees of competitors;
- mapping competitors' trade show attendance and advertising activities;
- setting up a database monitoring tenders;
- tracking changes in distribution;
- obtaining insights into competitors from common suppliers;
- building a database of all known current and former customers of competitors;
- tracking competitor pricing.

This list is by no means complete. Every organisation should determine which systems can be readily set up and maintained. It will then be essential to convince staff that the system is worth maintaining.

It is an inescapable fact that for systems to work it is essential for senior management to back them. The systems must then be seen to provide useful results.

USING OUTSIDERS

Acquirers can conduct CDD in-house. If consultants are to be used it is essential to get two things right:

- deciding when to use them;
- choosing who to use.

When to use outsiders

There are six fundamental reasons for using outsiders:

- 'We do not have sufficient internal resources to conduct the evaluation.'
- 'We lack knowledge which outsiders can bring.'
- 'We require a specific set of project management, investigative or analytical skills which outsiders can bring.'
- 'The evaluation is so important that we need increased credibility to sell it to the board.'
- 'We are not sure that we can remain objective, so we require an impartial view.'
- 'For reasons of confidentiality we cannot make all of the contacts and enquiries that we would like to on our own.'

Resources

At the time of an acquisition it is rare for a company to have sufficient spare resources which it can mobilise to cover all the necessary ground. Time is always limited, often to no more than a few weeks. Because of the level of potential risk in acquisitions, it is not acceptable to leave business or market areas insufficiently covered.

Knowledge

Outsiders are often hired for their knowledge of a particular industry, company or technology. If it is possible to find the right person or firm, this approach will yield excellent results. Large industries such as automotive, telecoms and chemicals are often supported by specialist firms or practice areas in larger consultancy firms which promote their sector knowledge.

The industry experts' knowledge should be more pertinent and detailed than that which can be developed by an industry outsider. Industry experts have a shallow learning curve and should know where to delve for information.

However, acquirers often overlook some of the downsides of turning to industry experts. While experts can claim an obvious head-start in an industry, they sometimes remain focused on their discipline and maintain contact with an unrepresentative sample of the industry with whom they have worked. They can provide highly partisan views. Industry experts often lack essential specific process skills such as the ability to obtain and analyse information in the context of an acquisition. The most dangerous of all can be so-called independent experts who used to work in the market but who are now losing touch with the industry.

At worst some can provide little more than the viewpoint of the single company for which they used to work.

When dealing with industry experts it is important to address the issue of confidentiality in detail. While it may be attractive to tap into a pool of knowledge, the client company must be concerned to ensure that confidentiality is preserved.

Skills

Experts in commercial due diligence should bring highly developed information-gathering and analytical skills.

Obtaining information from competitors is an excellent example of how consultants can add value. With a reasonable background knowledge of a target business CDD consultants can make a series of seemingly innocent enquiries which can lead to a detailed understanding of the strengths and weaknesses of a target company and its strategy. This work is invaluable in understanding the competitive environment before acquiring a company.

In the perhaps more mundane example of customers where the questions of access and confidentiality can be less difficult or critical, the process skills of commercial due diligence experts can be useful. A company's attitude towards its current customers tends to be customer-relationship or sales focused. An outsider is in a better position to discuss provider–customer relationships impartially. This helps to address the real issues which are driving the purchasing decision. This paves the way for the acquirer to understand the fundamental issues which are driving the market and the purchasing decision in the first instance; these are the issues which justify the very existence of the provider of products or services.

Outsiders can also obtain additional insights from the acquisition candidate itself.

The CDD team leader should meet with the top management of the seller independently of other elements of the due diligence programme. In fact any good CDD firm should recommend this approach. This meeting with top management is normally used to prepare the ground for customer interviews. The CDD firm can also use it to tease contacts and sensitive issues out of the seller. It also allows the CDD team to assess management – not just through this single meeting but through subsequent contact, particularly by gauging management reaction to problem areas which come to light, such as threatening market trends or problems with customers.

For example, a British specialist soft drinks company was negotiating with a venture capitalist. The CDD team met with management to set up the CDD programme. Management described strong growth in the German market and relatively slow sales in its domestic market. The CDD work in Germany revealed enormous demand and an unofficial German importer.

When challenged, the management admitted to encouraging four domestic wholesalers to open up unofficial channels into the German market due to a deteriorating relationship with its exclusive German distributor. This strong growth in Germany made the deal more attractive; the investigation also highlighted some of the post-acquisition integration actions.

Once high quality information has been gathered, the consultants you have hired should have the knowledge and experience required to select the best analytical tools which will provide a clear insight into the critical issues determining the outcome of the proposed business development initiative. Various approaches to analysis are set out in greater detail in Chapter 7.

Credibility

For major decisions a consultant's report can carry considerable weight. The board should be confident that, if correctly selected and briefed, the consultants will have addressed the problem in detail. This is not always the best reason for hiring outsiders, but it remains true that 'you cannot be fired for buying from IBM' (although perhaps the cliché should be updated to Microsoft!).

Objectivity

One of the best reasons to hire consultants is to ensure objectivity. Consultants should be judged on the quality of their information-gathering, analysis and conclusions. They should not be judged on the extent to which they agree with the personal agendas and viewpoints of managers. They should conduct their work objectively in the light of their client's corporate objectives; they should not bring personal agendas to bear.

Acquisitions can consume considerable amounts of managers' time. This often creates an onus for success as managers fear that colleagues may challenge their judgement for spending many months on a deal which does not lead to fruition. Equally acquisitions can change the shape and direction of companies. In any deal champions can, quite rightly, emerge for causes. Emotion can take over. In these circumstances the objectivity of outsiders such as non-executive directors and consultants is essential.

Confidentiality

In some cases an overriding argument for using outsiders is the need to maintain confidentiality. Consultants have the advantage of being divorced from their clients, therefore they can make general enquiries in a market about an acquisition candidate without raising any suspicion that the target may be for sale. Experienced commercial due diligence firms should have developed a wide range of approaches which allow them to maintain confidentiality while gathering incisive information through interviews.

If you are using consultants check their internal standards and procedures for confidentiality.

Selection criteria

In addition to the competence of the firm and its track record in commercial due diligence, two other important selection criteria for consultants should be considered:

- cost
- individual team members.

Cost

Inevitably, cost will always be an important selection criterion for consultants. It is important to select the right level of consultants for the task. Using market research firms for acquisition due diligence saves money, but can be dangerous as they will not always understand the full context of their enquiries. Using over-qualified consultants such as strategy firms rarely results in poor work, it is just very expensive.

Many consultancies will accept working on fixed-price contracts. For those few projects which are difficult to define at the outset and for which a 'taxi meter' approach is unavoidable, the buyer should set thresholds at which the consultancy will declare the current cost implication to its client.

It also makes sense to discuss expense limits in advance with consultants. These can often be capped.

Team members

It is always advisable to determine who the team members will be. Most senior partners of consulting firms can present themselves well and sell their firms effectively. What matters is who will do the work. Consultancies typically attract very talented staff; the trick is to ensure that the right balance of staff work on your assignment. Large firms will attempt to load as many of their junior staff as possible on to assignments, and while this has the benefit to the buyer of reducing the overall fee, it can lead to an indifferent result.

Ask who will be assigned to the project, check their credentials and ensure that any last-minute replacements are at least as well qualified.

If you are considering using one of the major accounting firms make sure that the team really are strategy or marketing experts – not former auditors who always start with and stick close to the numbers.

BRIEFING AND CONTROLLING OUTSIDERS

The quality of briefing has a significant impact on the quality of the consultant's report. The importance of addressing the seven critical questions from the outset was emphasised in Chapter 2. Make sure that any consultants you hire can answer the following questions:

- Why is our client planning to buy this company?
- Are we looking at the market, the company, management or all three?
- What are the parameters of the project?
- How do we handle any contact with the seller and its customers?
- What is our client's single most important objective?
- For whom in the client company are we doing this and how will the report be used?
- Are we to liaise with other due diligence teams?

Acquirers sometimes struggle when deciding how much information to share with consultants at the outset of a CDD programme. Broadly, there are three approaches:

- tell them nothing;
- provide selected information;
- share everything.

Share everything is best. However, depending on the circumstances of the commercial due diligence, one of the other two can be the right approach. The arguments for and against each of these approaches are set out below.

Tell them nothing

Organisations are tempted to tell consultants as little as possible for one or more of three reasons:

- they are highly paid and should work for their money;

- if they are so clever they should find all this out anyway;

- they will only regurgitate whatever we tell them in pretty charts and claim that they were the ones who found it out.

These are the wrong reasons. The right reason for providing commercial due diligence consultants with only the most basic profile of the assignment is that a fully impartial insight is required because there is a high level of internal debate and uncertainty or conflicting reports from the market which would make the briefings biased.

> For example, a British group planned to acquire a major North European consumer goods company. The level of interference of the supposedly non-executive chairman was a critical matter. The potential acquirer had very mixed reports. When briefing its specialist CDD firm about the chairman's role the acquirer raised the issue as one of concern, but did not reveal the information already held as it would cloud judgement. It transpired that the meddling non-executive chairman held a 'kitchen cabinet' in his own offices 20 times a year. This contradicted the company's official line that he simply attended eight board meetings a year.

Share everything

Typically it is best to share as much information as possible. This requires an initial level of trust between the consultancy firm and the client, the consultants being trusted not to 'borrow my watch, tell me the time and then give my watch to someone else'.

The advantages of sharing are:

- the consultants will not bill for their time spent reinventing the wheel;

- the consultants' approach will be better defined as it will be based on a clearer understanding of the issues;

- the consultants can make more practical recommendations as they understand the reasons for acquisition and the likely integration issues;

- the time taken to report back can possibly be reduced.

Although the bulk of any commercial due diligence programme must be based on enquiries external to the acquirer, sufficient time should be allowed to obtain internal information. Documents and opinions are best pooled from the outset. The quality of the overall result is not enhanced by a manager volunteering previously withheld detailed knowledge of the target or its market at a final presentation; this knowledge should have been fed into the process at an earlier point so it could be validated and developed.

It is best to share all information available across the various commercial, financial, legal and other due diligence teams. The project manager should ensure this information flow, possibly through a series of team meetings. Constant liaison between teams ensures that threats and opportunities identified by other investigations are taken into account.

It is useful to share contacts. Experienced consultants will ask whether their client has contacts within the target's customers and distributors, or any other contacts who can provide an insight to the company and market and how they can be used. They will also test which is the most fruitful approach to take to their enquiries in the market.

Provide selected information

There can also be a half-way house in information-sharing. In some commercial due diligence programmes it makes sense to wait until the interim point before providing all the detail held internally. The first phase may have been used to assess the credibility of alternative business development routes to an acquisition. Then further detail can be provided allowing detailed analysis of the options, including acquisitions.

> For example, a market-leading floor coverings manufacturer suffering from rapidly declining sales in a core market needed to evaluate an acquisition opportunity in a related market. The company provided little initial information when briefing its advisors to investigate the problem in its core market as it required a fully independent evaluation of the market. It needed to find out in detail its competitors' market shares, by market segment. Once this information had been gathered independently the company released all the collaborating market data that it held to allow a detailed analysis of the market size and segmentation. The conclusion was that the market leader was performing in line with the market – which was going through a period of unprecedented change and decline. The proposed acquisition would add little value. The acquisition plan and capital investment decisions were consequently revised.

DANGER SIGNS

Using consultants can be an expensive way of failing to solve a problem. Some danger signs to watch out for are set out in Table 11.1.

Table 11.1 Managing consultants – danger signs

- Failure to ask searching questions during briefing

  The consultants may not be thinking through their approach.

- Failure to discuss confidentiality

  Confidentiality procedures may be weak.

- Emphasis on previous sector experience

  Possible over-selling of experience: how real is it and will the individuals with the experience be on the project?

- Team changes

  Lack of continuity during the process; other assignments may be more important to the consultancy; junior staff are being assigned to your project.

- Process appears 'off the shelf'

  The consultancy may not have thought through how to adapt its approach to your market.

- Difficult to contact senior team members

  They may be busy on other projects, leaving the work to juniors.

- Lack of proactive issue raising

  Possible limited ongoing analysis and ability to understand the business.

- Customers annoyed during 'customer care' programme

  The consultants are applying their process insensitively.

Table 11.1 is not intended to be exhaustive. Keep in regular contact with the consultants so you can spot danger signs such as these and others.

12

Vendor due diligence

WHAT IS VENDOR DUE DILIGENCE?

Vendor due diligence (VDD) is the name for any due diligence reports which are commissioned by the current owners of the business in preparation for their sale. Financial reports can be commissioned at this stage as well as commercial reports.

Vendor due diligence is relatively new. The growth in its use coincided with the sellers' market of the late 1990s, particularly as astute advisors who manage auctions sought to take control of the due diligence process.

ADVANTAGES FOR THE SELLER

Buyers conduct due diligence because they want to reduce risk and obtain a negotiating advantage. Vendor due diligence turns the tables as it favours the seller far more than the buyer. Some sellers commission VDD as they are genuinely trying to reveal all the bad news so its discovery later is not used as an excuse to chisel the price down. However, buyers who are confronted with a prepackaged report presented by the seller should be wary. Even if the independent organisation which conducted the work has the highest reputation it will have been briefed by the seller and it will not have been encouraged to expose potential weaknesses to their full. If the vendor due diligence is presented as a fait accompli the buyer can feel powerless to obtain the quality of insight it would normally expect when planning an acquisition.

HOW THE BUYER CAN FIND THE TRUE PICTURE

So, if vendor due diligence is potentially flawed what can the buyer do about it? Checklist 12.1 sets out some guidelines.

Checklist 12.1 How to assess the validity of a vendor due diligence report

Issue	Implication
Who did the work?	
■ Strategy firm	Quality and neutrality of output should both be good.
■ Accounting firm	Quality will be restricted by financial culture and lack of depth in the commercial terms of reference. Fear of litigation will make the report neutral, to the point of being bland.

■ CDD specialist	Quality and neutrality of the output will probably be good.
■ Other firm	Uncertain quality due to lack of CDD culture; possible lack of focus on competitive position and management; some small firms may be influenced by the seller.

Will the seller allow you to contact the firm?

■ No	Be very cautious of the report.
■ Yes	Can be useful.

Ask the firm

■ Was your bill paid in full?	A consultancy should not accept its report being directed or rewritten by its client – this can lead to conflict, to the point of not being paid in full.
■ Did you fall out with your client?	What were the issues which the client saw as positive but the consultancy saw as negative?
■ What had to be reworded/redrafted and what was deleted?	
■ How many draft reports were there?	The more drafts, the less you should believe the report.
■ Would you buy the company? (Emphasise that the question is 'off the record' particularly when dealing with the major accounting firms.)	How does that compare to what is written in the report?
■ What are the greatest challenges facing the business?	Are there 'real' issues not in the report?

Further work

■ Would a limited 'top-up' exercise be possible?	Provides the opportunity to address any unresolved concerns.

In extreme cases sceptical purchasers commission their own independent commercial investigations. This has inevitable difficulties as the seller will see little need to co-operate, arguing that the ground has already been covered satisfactorily. The seller may deny access to management and word the confidentiality agreement to forbid customer and distributor interviews.

CONCLUSION

Vendor due diligence severely restricts the purchaser's room for manoeuvre. With active management it is possible to find some ways around these restrictions, but the outcome is never as satisfactory as when the purchaser has control of the process.

13

Conclusion

Commercial due diligence helps the acquirer to take an acquisition decision. It also informs his valuation, negotiation and integration. Figure 13.1 sets out the role of CDD.

Fig. 13.1 Role of commercial due diligence

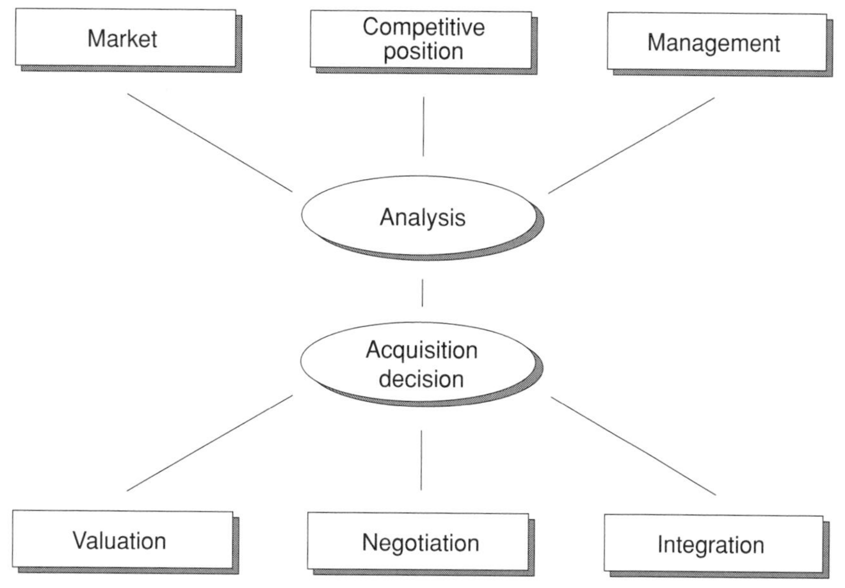

© AMR, 1991.   Reproduced with the permission of AMR International Limited.

A sound commercial due diligence programme requires:

- a clearly defined and well understood goal – so the team can focus and use its initiative;

- a well considered but flexible methodology – covering all the areas of risk and reacting to developments;

- the right team and resources – use outsiders when necessary;

- effective project management – co-ordinating resources and focusing on the issues;

- information quality which corresponds to the scale of the acquisition – seek out the best published and unpublished information;

- a structured approach to plugging information gaps – create a framework for assumptions supporting each argument and highlight weaknesses;

- clear but simple analysis – choose the most appropriate analytical tool;

- a straightforward conclusion – answer the chairman's question 'Would you put your own money into this?'

Case study – Playco

You are the chief executive of a UK plc involved in the development, manufacture and sale of high-technology equipment for the packaging industry. You are attracted to an acquisition opportunity which appears to have a good fit with your core business. Playco, the acquisition candidate, is represented by Flogemoff, a corporate finance advisor, which presented the company in its glowing memorandum as follows.

PRESENTATION OF THE COMPANY

Background

Playco is a fast growing private company which supplies:

- marking and coding equipment to the packaging industry for the overprinting of sell-by dates and other codes;
- metal detectors for contaminant detection on food production and packaging lines.

Playco is owned and managed by its directors. The founder and managing director Andy Large is the majority owner.

Through technical innovation and software strength Playco has been catapulted to success with its Smoothprint range of thermal marking and coding products. The Detectex metal detection product, which was launched two and a half years ago, claims technical leadership. Playco's rapid sales growth is forecast to continue with sales doubling over the next two years. The driver for this growth is the lean but effective R&D team which has won numerous industry awards, most recently for the rapid development of Playco's new Smoothprint product.

The business was founded ten years ago by Andy and a colleague who left three years later. There are three non-executive directors; each owns 6 per cent of Playco.

Reason for sale

Playco requires a stronger capital base and effective international distribution to achieve its full potential.

The company has achieved a significant UK market share in marking and coding by quickly replacing the outdated stamping technology on existing packaging lines in its chosen FMCG customer base. In metal detection Playco also has a leading product which sells into the same market. Andy and his team now recognise that they need to achieve effective international distribution and market coverage to maintain their rate of growth and avoid stagnation as the UK markets for both product lines become increasingly saturated.

Manufacturing

Until 18 months ago, Playco manufactured nothing itself and subcontracted all assembly to two external suppliers, Playco retaining responsibility for procurement and ultimate quality control. As the production process for metal detectors is relatively simple, in-house assembly was started one year after the product launch. There are no current plans to bring Smoothprint production in-house. Through this subcontract policy Playco has been able to remain flexible during its expansion providing it with a demonstrable competitive advantage and a limited overhead.

Facilities

Playco outgrew its old building last year and six months ago moved into purpose-built leasehold premises on a nearby business park. Although it fills only approximately 50,000 square feet of the 80,000 square feet available in the new premises, Playco's board felt it important to build in capacity for the aggressive expansion it anticipates. There were a number of one-off costs associated with the move, including professional expenses, removals and IT upgrades, amounting in total to £250,000, which has been written off against the current year's profit.

Financial performance

Playco's recent financial performance shows sales doubling over two years to £11.2m; profits have nearly tripled over the same period to £2.5m.

Sales are split as follows:	£m
Smoothprint	6.0
Smoothprint consumables	2.2
Detectex	3.0

Offers for the business

Playco represents an excellent acquisition opportunity for a business seeking entry into a fast growing and highly profitable niche of the packaging industry. As the three non-executive members of Playco's board wish to retire at completion, the shareholders are unanimous that the purchase consideration will be payable in full at legal completion, with no earn-out.

In a first attempt to see through some of the sales puff you telephone Flogemoff, Playco's corporate finance advisor, and obtain the following further insights.

Further issues raised by Playco's corporate finance advisor

■ Andy Large is only 35, but he is widely recognised in the industry as having a rare mix of talents combining commercial and R&D skills. Along with general management, Andy oversees product development and marketing.

■ Andy attributes much of the early success of the business to the involvement of three local businessmen, who provided start-up capital when he founded the company and have provided helpful advice and useful contacts over the years.

■ This enabled Andy and his team to avoid many of the mistakes commonly found in developing businesses and to accelerate the growth of Playco beyond what they could have achieved on their own. Andy has always been happy to pay these three non-executive directors generously, at the rate of £30,000 per annum, for the time they contribute at board meetings but also in recognition of their help in the early days.

■ Because of the cash generative nature of the business, Andy had not felt the need to employ a financial director until 12 months ago. Up till then Playco relied instead on a quarterly management accounts pack, prepared by the company's auditors with the help of Playco's full-time financial controller. Ray

Bowley was appointed as finance director one year ago. He joined from Cintel, a metal detection competitor.

- No detailed profitability analysis is available for the three main revenue streams. Given the company's growth and overall profitability this has seemed unnecessary to date.

- Playco's growth has attracted the attention of a number of potential acquirers. Many of them are expanding quoted companies with a desire to make acquisitions and fuel eps growth, but with few commercial benefits to offer Playco. However, five groups, including yours, are potentially of interest because they operate in related market areas, share some customers with Playco, and appear to offer the international marketing platform Playco needs.

Visiting Playco

Having read the brief description of Playco prepared by the vendor's advisors and heard some more positive sales talk from them on the telephone, you arrange to meet the management team. This was essential as you need to see through the sales talk and get a feel for the operation by meeting Andy and his team.

At the meeting with Andy Large, Ray Bowley and two other senior colleagues, you received an impressive presentation 'from the horse's mouth'. This was followed by a tour of Playco's facility. This confirmed your view that although small in a global context, the business appears to be 'world class'. Other salient points that came from your day with Andy and his team include the following:

- There is an abundance of space to expand in their new premises.

- Prudent spending on R&D has, in the past, always produced opportunities to develop and market new products. Nothing is included, even in their plan, for any new products which may result from current R&D spending. Some results are anticipated particularly from an X-ray contaminant detection system. The impact on Playco's profits from this and any other products would be a 'windfall' above the current forecast.

- A number of 'ground breaking' large orders for Smoothprint are now on the horizon from major European food manufacturers which have been using Playco's products on trial for several months.

- One of the major motivations for the transaction, apart from realising value for the shareholders, is Andy's desire to continue developing his career within a larger organisation and take on the greater challenges that this will bring.

- Ray, the finance director, was taciturn during the meeting. Other members of the management team appear to be independent thinkers, but with great loyalty to Andy.

- Management accounts appear to confirm that the current year trading is as forecast and that next year's budget is achievable, using Playco's existing sales channels. But Andy is convinced that with your sizeable international distribution network and established customer relationships worldwide that the next year's budgeted pre-tax profit of £2.6m plus could be significantly exceeded. This prospect is tantalising.

- There has been demonstrable interest shown by several of your competitors and the thought that one of them may acquire Playco makes you shudder because losing this acquisition would be a major setback to your industrial policy and acquisition strategy.

Offer made and accepted

You are impressed by the business and make an offer of £15m–£17m; you consider the lower end of the range to be a very full offer. You are told that the seller expects that your final offer will come in at the top end of the range. Nonetheless you secure access to the business for a period of four weeks' due diligence, by the end of which you must confirm the actual price you will pay for Playco.

Although acutely aware of the significance of this deal, your board is concerned not to overpay.

As so much depends on Playco's potential growth and as the management structure appears thin you decide to conduct commercial due diligence. This will be the key to assessing the true value of Playco to your business …

COMMERCIAL DUE DILIGENCE PROGRAMME

You agree a brief with an agency specialising in CDD. It is as follows.

Market

- What are the drivers in Playco's markets?
- What are the underlying trends in the markets?

Competitive position

- How do Playco's market share and profit levels compare to rivals?
- Will they improve or deteriorate?
- Are there major threats or new entrants on the horizon?

■ Will Playco's competitive position be enhanced when integrated into our existing business?

Management

■ How solid is Playco's management structure?
■ How reliable is Andy Large?

Interview programme

The CDD agency responds to your briefing. After a rapid review of desk research materials it sets up and conducts an interview programme. It interviews:

■ Management:
  – Andy Large
■ Thermal marking and coding market participants:
  – major Playco customers
  – Playco distributors outside the UK
  – competitors in stamping (the old-fashioned rival technology)
  – competitors in thermal (direct competitors to Playco)
  – the recently-ousted founder of Counter (market leader in thermal)
  – packaging equipment OEMs (on whose equipment Playco's machines sit)
  – suppliers of consumables (inked ribbons)
■ Metal detection market participants:
  – major Playco customers
  – Playco distributors outside the UK
  – competitors
  – suppliers of corollary products – checkweighers
■ Internal contacts (i.e. within acquirer):
  – senior management
  – international subsidiaries and distributors.

COMMERCIAL DUE DILIGENCE PROGRAMME RESULTS

Additional information uncovered by CDD firm at meeting with Playco

The CDD agency's meeting with Andy Large and Ray Bowley reveals information which the acquirer had not obtained. This includes:

- the founder of Counter and inventor of thermal technology has just left Counter after a falling-out (he was added to the interview programme);
- there are no indigenous US competitors in thermal marking and coding;
- a US study of the US thermal marking and coding market was commissioned by Playco last year, but Andy Large refused to disclose it;
- although Playco claims to be technical leader in metal detection, there is little to differentiate the technology of metal detection competitors;
- price is becoming increasingly important in metal detection.

Data from interviews

The following data emerged from interviews with market participants.

Market status – thermal coding and marking

- This market is a separate niche to the better known ink-jet coding market.
- The market for thermal coders is currently based on the retrofit of stamping machines, which are now often replaced before the end of their lives due to the technical superiority of thermal technology.
- Consumables are considerable expenditure items. Users can easily purchase thermal ribbons on the open market, whereas stamping ribbons are mostly purchased from the machine manufacturer – this threatens Playco's consumables sales volumes.
- Over half of the stamping market is linked to vertical form fill seal machines (VFFS), a type of packaging equipment. Therefore the trends within the VFFS market are essential to the growth of thermal technology.
- The introduction of thermal technology has grown the market for coding machines due to its impressive technical characteristics.
- Laser technology may threaten thermal if its price disadvantage is reduced.

Further interviews were conducted with manufacturers of VFFS machines. These revealed the following.

■ The VFFS market is set to grow at 5–10 per cent p.a.

Conclusion: Thermal technology has grown the coding market. It will replace over half of the demand for stamping within eight years of introduction (see Figure A1.1).

Fig. A1.1 New sales into 100 UK stamping applications

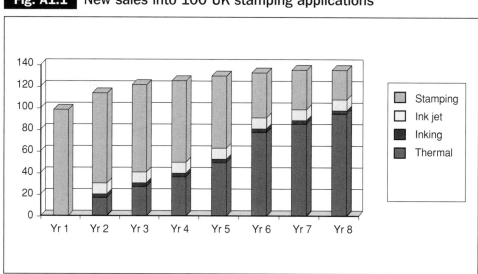

Competitive position – thermal coding and marking

■ Counter was the first entrant and is market leader; in fact Playco has copied Counter's product. It risked patent infringement but Counter's legal case against Playco failed by a narrow margin.

■ Counter is owned by a major US group, IWT, which also owns the US leader in stamping; but the two companies do not co-operate and Counter has virtually no sales in the US. Counter's management appears mediocre.

■ Playco sells its equipment at a 10–20 per cent discount over Counter. However, thermal technology is 80–100 per cent more expensive than stamping.

■ Playco has a 'hard sell' reputation; there is little evidence of its ability to provide support. Some customers complain of 'hit and run' selling.

■ Playco has a 34 per cent market share. Other competitors are later entrants and less well focused than Playco.

- The major stamping companies have mismanaged their development of thermal technology, mostly as they remain overly focused on their increasingly old-fashioned technologies.

- A US competitor in thermal technology is developing its business rapidly in one user segment, despite Andy Large's assertion that there are no US competitors.

- Playco is set to win major US accounts but has little distribution to support its success.

- VFFS OEMs are not aligned to stamping or to thermal technology as most users specify their printing equipment preference. Nonetheless, Playco is well regarded among OEMs.

- Recent price rises announced by Playco for ribbons and replacement print heads have caused consternation among many customers who have started to look elsewhere for consumables.

- Playco had previously attempted to sell itself to an ink-jet company (with which it conducted the US market report that Andy refused to hand over). It is not clear why these negotiations collapsed.

Conclusion: Smoothprint's market share is set to increase, but the aggressive sales-driven expansion strategy is unsustainable within the current structure, particularly in the US.

Market status – metal detection

- Historical growth in the UK metal detector market of 15 per cent p.a. has now slowed to 8 per cent p.a.

- Now that the venture capital owners of market leader Safeflow have sold out to the US checkweigher giant Cleveland Metal every metal detection company is owned by or aligned with a checkweighing company.

- In over 60 per cent of cases buyers replace checkweighers and metal detectors simultaneously.

- As the cost of X-ray detection systems continues to plummet, X-ray system suppliers claim that they will take share from traditional metal detectors.

- GEG is investing £500m in its X-ray business, in part at least to challenge traditional metal detectors.

- Playco has an estimated 6 per cent market share.

> *Conclusion: Metal detection is a competitive market with little room for niche players. The market is becoming increasingly aligned with that of checkweighing.*

Competitive position – metal detectors

- Playco is rated as a niche player. Andy Large has used his personality and contacts to sell Detectex to some Smoothprint customers.

- Users are unaware of any particular technical advantage offered by Detectex.

- Price is the only advantage Detectex has over the market leader Safeflow and others.

- Detectex is compatible with checkweighers, which work in conjunction with metal detectors, but Detectex lacks the ease of interface offered by other metal detectors.

- Some customers complained of late delivery and poor calibration causing inaccurate detection and numerous false alarms.

- Playco had attempted to sell Detectex products through its international Smoothprint distributors. This failed as different departments within end users are responsible for coding and detection purchasing.

- The German distributor plans to drop Detectex due to product unreliability and a row with Ray Bowley over payment terms.

> *Conclusion: Detectex is a me-too product launched into a competitive market. Playco needs a strategic alliance with a checkweighing company to build critical mass ahead of industry consolidation.*

Management

- Andy Large's father died at 45, as did his grandfather. Andy is rumoured to be selling the business so he can cash in for an early pension.

- Andy Large has an excellent reputation as a manager, but he can be abrasive.

- Ray Bowley left Cintel after an unexpected dip in profits.

- There is little further depth of management at Playco.

Conclusion: Playco's culture is entrepreneurial. Andy Large is critical to the company, but it is not clear to what extent he can be relied on after the deal has been concluded. Ray Bowley may not be solid.

Using the information

The quality of insight provided by the commercial due diligence investigation allows you to:

- draw up a SWOT analysis (*see* Figure A1.2);
- use the data gathered to forecast Playco's performance with a reasonable degree of comfort by feeding it into your valuation model;
- make a revised offer based on a concrete understanding of the business;
- plan integration actions such as:
  - strengthened new management structure
  - clearly defined role for Andy Large in the group
  - integrated US distribution
  - improved quality control
  - revised consumables pricing policy
  - European distribution review
  - checkweigher product development/partnership
  - possible Smoothprint price rise
  - feasibility study for continuing X-ray development
  - in-house Smoothprint assembly;
- manage the negotiations with the seller by feeding in those negative aspects of the business which were uncovered.

Fig. A1.2 Playco SWOT

Strengths	Weaknesses
• Andy Large • Smoothprint technology • Smoothprint price position • Sales skills • UK reference sites	• Detectex product faults • International distribution • Smoothprint consumables price • Lack of checkweigh product • Administration • Management depth • Development resources for X-ray
Opportunities	**Threats**
• Develop US Smoothprint market • Further penetrate stamping market • Develop a checkweighing product • Partner with checkweighing company • Take assembly in-house • Discount Smoothprint less • Offer other complementary products	• Detectex squeezed in consolidating market • Loss of Smoothprint consumables • Thermal competitors discount • X-ray supersedes metal detection

Conclusion

Table A1.1 compares the picture of the business provided by Flogemoff to the understanding you gained through CDD. While Flogemoff provided correct information it was either optimistic or it addressed issues which were not critical to the business.

Table A1.1 Playco: comparison of presentations

Playco as presented by Flogemoff	Playco as found through CDD
Innovative	Yes, but Smoothprint is a copy of Counter's product and Playco risked patent infringement. Detectex is no more than a me-too product. Playco has focused development on X-ray, when it would have been better off developing a checkweighing product. Playco cannot compete with GEG's level of development on its £500m X-ray business. Playco has no plans to develop laser technology. The major ink-jet players are investing heavily in laser as it may allow them to target wider markets, including thermal.

Table A1.1 Continued

High growth	Yes, thermal has expanded the market, but some growth has been achieved by aggressive selling and discounting. This position may not be sustainable.
	In fact, the thermal market is driven by VFFS; fortunately this market has a healthy outlook.
	Consumables sales for thermal coders will not grow as users can find inexpensive supplies on the open market.
	Growth is slowing in the European metal detection market. Playco is poorly positioned to benefit from growth elsewhere in the world.
	The product fit between thermal and metal detection is questionable. Often different buyers and engineers are responsible for the products.
US opportunity	Yes, Counter takes no advantage of its US parent organisation's channels.
	But there is a fast-growing domestic US competitor in thermal coding and marking.
	Also Playco has no infrastructure to sell and support Smoothprint in the US.
	Detectex lacks the critical mass necessary to be viable in the US.
Few European thermal competitors	Yes, but only because the stamping competitors mismanaged their reaction to thermal. They will now enter the market late.
	Playco entered the thermal market by copying a rival's product. Other new entrants could do likewise.
Management strength	Yes, Andy Large has fostered a highly entrepreneurial culture. But he is rumoured to be selling for personal reasons and may not remain with the business.
	Andy dominates his team and may be difficult to contain on your board.
	Ray Bowley left Cintel under a cloud and his department is prone to making mistakes.
	There is little management depth.
Highly profitable	Yes, the figures prove it.
	But profits are generated mostly by thermal consumables and thermal coders. The consumables market is under threat due to price rises and ease of substitution.
	The coder market may mature and stamping competitors may enter it, again reducing Playco's profits.
	Playco can make little profit in metal detection. Playco's position in this market is weakening and profitability can only decline.